THROUGH a GLASS DARKLY
The Psychological Effects
of
Marijuana
and
Hashish

THE ENCYCLOPEDIA OF
PSYCHOLOGICAL DISORDERS

Senior Consulting Editor Carol C. Nadelson, M.D.
Consulting Editor Claire E. Reinburg

THROUGH a GLASS DARKLY
The Psychological Effects
of
Marijuana
and
Hashish

Elizabeth Russell Connelly

CHELSEA HOUSE PUBLISHERS
Philadelphia

The ENCYCLOPEDIA OF PSYCHOLOGICAL DISORDERS provides up-to-date information on the history of, causes and effects of, and treatment and therapies for problems affecting the human mind. The titles in this series are not intended to take the place of the professional advice of a psychiatrist or mental health care professional.

Chelsea House Publishers
Editor in Chief: Stephen Reginald
Managing Editor: James D. Gallagher
Production Manager: Pamela Loos
Art Director: Sara Davis
Director of Photography: Judy L. Hasday
Senior Production Editor: Lisa Chippendale

Staff for THE PSYCHOLOGICAL EFFECTS OF MARIJUANA AND HASHISH
Editorial Assistant: Heather Forkos, Lily Sprague
Picture Researcher: Sandy Jones
Associate Art Director: Takeshi Takahashi
Designer: Brian Wible
Cover Design: Brian Wible

The ChelseaHouse World Wide Web site address is
http://www.chelseahouse.com

Library of Congress Cataloging-in-Publication Data

Connelly, Elizabeth.
Through a glass darkly : the psychological effects of marijuana and hashish / by Elizabeth Russell Connelly.
p. cm. — (Encyclopedia of psychological disorders)
Includes bibliographical references and index.
Summary: Examines the history, use, and mental and psychological effects of marijuana and hashish, as well as their impact on society and current treatment for their abuse.
ISBN 0-7910-4897-7 (hc)
1. Marijuana—Psychological aspects—Juvenile literature. 2. Hashish—Psychological aspects—Juvenile literature. [1. Marijuana. 2. Hashish. 3. Drug Abuse.] I. Title. II. Series.
HV5822.M3C64 1998
362.29'5—dc21

                                                                        98-34150
                                                                           CIP
                                                                            AC

CONTENTS

PSYCHOLOGICAL DISORDERS AND THEIR EFFECT

CAROL C. NADELSON, M.D.
PRESIDENT AND CHIEF EXECUTIVE OFFICER,
The American Psychiatric Press

There are a wide range of problems that are considered psychological disorders, including mental and emotional disorders, problems related to alcohol and drug abuse, and some diseases that cause both emotional and physical symptoms. Psychological disorders often begin in early childhood, but during adolescence we see a sharp increase in the number of people affected by these disorders. It has been estimated that about 20 percent of the U.S. population will have some form of mental disorder sometime during their lifetime. Some psychological disorders appear following severe stress or trauma. Others appear to occur more often in some families and may have a genetic or inherited component. Still other disorders do not seem to be connected to any cause we can yet identify. There has been a great deal of attention paid to learning about the causes and treatments of these disorders, and exciting new research has taught us a great deal in the last few decades.

The fact that many new and successful treatments are available makes it especially important that we reject old prejudices and outmoded ideas that consider mental disorders to be untreatable. If psychological problems are identified early, it is possible to prevent serious consequences. We should not keep these problems hidden or feel shame that we or a member of our family has a mental disorder. Some people believe that something they said or did caused a mental disorder. Some people think that these disorders are "only in your head" so that you could "snap out of it" if you made the effort. This type of thinking implies that a treatment is a matter of willpower or motivation. It is a terrible burden for someone who is suffering to be blamed for their misery, and often people with psychological disorders are not treated compassionately. We hope that the information in this book will teach you about various mental illnesses.

The problems covered in the volumes in the ENCYCLOPEDIA OF PSYCHOLOGICAL DISORDERS were selected because they are of particular importance to young adults, because they affect them directly or because they affect family and friends. There are individual volumes on reading disorders, attention deficit and disruptive behavior disorders, and dementia—all of these are related to our abilities to learn and integrate information from the world around us. There are books on drug abuse that provide useful information about the effects of these drugs and treatments that are available for those individuals who have drug problems. Some of the books concentrate on one of the most common mental disorders, depression. Others deal with eating disorders, which are dangerous illnesses that affect a large number of young adults, especially women.

Most of the public attention paid to these disorders arises from a particular incident involving a celebrity that awakens us to our own vulnerability to psychological problems. These incidents of celebrities or public figures revealing their own psychological problems can also enable us to think about what we can do to prevent and treat these types of problems.

OVERVIEW: ADOLESCENTS AND DRUG USE

Adolescence, that sometimes turbulent stretch between the ages of 13 and 18, is a critical period of accelerated hormonal changes, personality development, and identity formation. These rapidly changing states can cause adolescents to feel awkward, insecure, and inadequate about their appearance and popularity. Popularity among peers is especially important for many teens. They want to be accepted, complimented, and approved of by their classmates. They want to fit in.

For many, adolescence is a time of frustration, anger, and rebellion. This is a period in adolescents' lives when they are more likely to test limits and manipulate others, often experimenting with extreme behavior and values. Adolescents can be confused and scared, and they sometimes exhibit much internal conflict: one minute they may demand total independence, and the next they seem desperate for protection from the world around them.

It is also a period of endless exploration, when risk-taking and sensation-seeking are provocative steps on the path to self-discovery. For many adolescents, experimentation with drugs, including marijuana and hashish, is part of growing up. In a nationwide study conducted by the National Institute on Drug Abuse (NIDA), 45 percent of high school seniors report having used illicit drugs at least once, and 30 percent acknowledge having used them before high school. Concern arises from the fact that regular and addictive use of drugs, especially during adolescence, can cause problems with psychological, emotional, and social development.

There is evidence that experimentation with and regular use of alcohol and other drugs during adolescence follows a certain pattern. The most frequently used psychoactive substance among adolescents is alcohol. In the case of teens who try other drugs, there appears to be a general progression of substance involvement, from use of beer or wine, to cigarettes, to marijuana, and to other drugs such as heroin and cocaine. Of course, the "progression of use" concept isn't a hard-and-fast rule; there are always exceptions, such as the adolescent who starts with crack cocaine without trying cigarettes or marijuana first.

One study shows that in the United States, the average age for initial experimentation with tobacco and alcohol is usually 12 years, with marijuana and hashish use typically beginning about two years later (Mezzich et al., 1994). Within these general age-related substance use patterns, several gender-related differences also have been found. For example, the tendency to smoke cigarettes is higher in teenage girls than in boys. In contrast, young men are 40 percent more likely than young women to consume marijuana daily. Also, the average age for initially qualifying for a diagnosis of a psychoactive substance use disorder (PSUD) for alcohol or drug abuse/dependence is slightly older in young women. Once they've started using drugs, however, young women appear to progress faster to a diagnosis of PSUD than young men, and they more rapidly develop problems connected to alcohol and drug use. One positive sign is that young women also tend to seek treatment sooner than young men (Mezzich et al., 1994).

In the United States, the legalization of marijuana—suggested for every purpose from greater social harmony to alleviating medical problems—continues to be a hot topic. This book does not attempt to argue whether or not cannabis (the plant from which marijuana and hashish are prepared) should be legalized, for medical use or otherwise. Rather, its goal is to introduce middle, junior high, and high school students to the effects of marijuana and hashish on the human mind.

Chapter 1 provides an overview, introducing readers to the world of marijuana and hashish. Chapter 2 traces the history of cannabis to provide some perspective on issues surrounding the drug today. Chapter 3 offers some explanations for what prompts adolescents to use drugs in the first place. Then, Chapter 4 delves deeper into the concepts introduced in Chapter 1 to explain how individuals might be affected when they use marijuana. Chapter 5 looks at the bigger picture to analyze the impact of marijuana and hashish on society. Finally, Chapter 6 highlights the most commonly used methods for treating problems associated with use of these drugs today.

Cannabis is the most widely used illicit drug in the United States. Approximately five percent of the U.S. population (10.1 million people) are current marijuana users, according to the 1996 National Household Survey on Drug Abuse.

USE THIS →

1

A POPULAR POISON

Marijuana and hashish are the most frequently used illicit substances among adolescents. Current estimates indicate that approximately one-third of U.S. high school seniors and about one-quarter of the grade 13 students in Ontario, Canada, have tried these substances at least once, and that nearly five percent of U.S. high school seniors use marijuana or hashish daily. Although this level of use is significantly below the peak that occurred in the late 1970s, marijuana use has risen significantly among U.S. high school students since 1992. There is also a marked increase in the drug's use among students in seventh and eighth grades (Duffy and Milin, 1996).

Use of marijuana and hashish can vary from experimentation to abuse to chronic use. Though generally few long-term effects have been found to afflict most users, chronic use may result in behavioral and psychological problems. It is believed that use of these substances in early adolescence tends to lead to later exploration of other, more potent drugs, such as cocaine, crack, heroin, and lysergic acid diethylamide (LSD). And depending on the amount and frequency of cannabis use, a person can experience a variety of symptoms, some of which can lead to diagnosis of a psychological disorder. The American Psychiatric Association (APA) recognizes a number of cannabis-induced disorders that may be caused by heavy use; these disorders are described in greater detail in Chapter 4.

Despite—or perhaps because of—its popularity and history, cannabis evokes quite a controversy. Proponents of the legalization of the drug range from those who want marijuana to gain acceptance for its myriad medicinal uses to those who believe the drug can contribute to social harmony. Opponents of widespread cannabis use and legalization generally point to the drug's addictive qualities as an inherent danger and note its role as a "gateway" to harder drugs.

The plant cannabis sativa *has been used for both medicinal and recreational purposes for centuries. The plant originated in central Asia but is now found in many parts of the world.*

USE This →

WHAT ARE MARIJUANA AND HASHISH?

USE This

Cannabis, from which marijuana and hashish are made, is one of the oldest drugs known. Cannabis has been documented as both a medicinal and a recreational substance since ancient times.

Marijuana and hashish are made up of cannabinoids, or substances derived from the cannabis plant. When the upper leaves, flowering tops, seeds, and stems of the plant are cut and dried, the product is usually called marijuana. In the West, marijuana is typically rolled into cigarettes, called "joints." It can also be ingested orally—a method popular in Asia. The most potent form of marijuana available in the United States today is called "sensimilla." Hashish, commonly called "hash," is the sticky resin that seeps from the marijuana plant's flowering tops and the undersides of its leaves; hashish oil is a more potent, concentrated distillate of hashish. Usually smoked in a pipe or bong, hash can also be taken orally and is sometimes mixed with tea or food, such as brownies.

The cannabinoid identified as primarily responsible for the psychoactive effects of cannabis is THC (delta-9-tetrahydrocannabinol, or delta-9 THC). It is rarely available for use in a pure form. Though THC content varies greatly, the percentage in marijuana has increased significantly since the late 1960s—from an average of approximately one to five percent to as much as 10 to 15 percent. Relative to marijuana, hashish typically contains a higher percentage of THC (Frances and Franklin, 1994). Synthetic delta-9-THC is sometimes used for such medical purposes as alleviating the nausea and vomiting caused by chemotherapy or anorexia and the weight loss resulting from acquired immunodeficiency syndrome (AIDS).

USE THIS ✗

Street names for marijuana and common terms for various marijuana cigarettes include the following:

street NAMES

Marijuana street names: pot, doob, grass, reefer, weed, tea, MJ, and maryjane; *HEMP, MARY JANE*

Marijuana forms and terms: joint (marijuana cigarette); kiff (marijuana and tobacco); roach (butt end of joint); A-bomb (marijuana and heroin); AMP (marijuana and formaldehyde); supergrass (marijuana and PCP); illy (marijuana, formaldehyde, methanol, and PCP); and primos (marijuana and crack cocaine).

HOW ARE USERS AFFECTED?

Individuals who regularly use cannabis often report both physical and mental lethargy. They tend to feel somewhat detached from themselves and their surroundings and experience time as passing slowly. Mild forms of depression, anxiety, or irritability are seen in about one-third of those who use cannabis daily or almost daily. When taken in

USE
THIS

Mild forms of depression, anxiety, or irritability are common side effects of chronic marijuana use. High doses of marijuana can cause a distorted sense of time, loss of short-term memory, hallucinations, and loss of balance.

high doses, cannabinoids have psychoactive effects that can be similar to those of hallucinogens (drugs that cause hallucinations) such as LSD. Also, persons who use marijuana or hashish can experience adverse mental effects that resemble hallucinogen-induced "bad trips." These range from mild to moderate levels of anxiety—for example, over the concern that police will discover the drugs—to severe anxiety reactions resembling panic attacks. Demonstration of paranoia is also a possible side effect, ranging from suspiciousness to extreme delusions and hallucinations.

CASE STUDY: LISA

The following case of a young woman at a hospital emergency room illustrates some of the psychological complications that can result from marijuana use:

Sixteen-year-old Lisa has been suffering from insomnia and the troubling feeling that a neighbor is out to get her. Her mother accompanies her to the hospital and reports the occurrence of auditory and visual hallucinations.

Lisa's home life is apparently stable: she is the younger of two children and reportedly gets along well with her older brother and other family members. Lisa's mother provides some evidence that discipline is not firm and that Lisa may be a somewhat spoiled child. However, she does well in school and has many friends.

Prior to her hallucinations and sleeplessness, Lisa had been smoking two joints daily for about two months and had stopped 48 hours before her symptoms began. She had also broken up with her boyfriend of nine months at the same time.

Neither Lisa nor her family has any history of serious illness or emotional problems. Lisa herself attributes her symptoms to the possibility that she "smoked too much herb." On the evening before her hallucinations, she began to experience an odd feeling that unusual events were occurring at the home of a friend, whom she knew was in an abusive relationship. Lisa developed the delusion that her friend had been killed by the abusive boyfriend and that the body was in the house. Upon seeing the woman alive the next day, she became confused.

Lisa also developed the persistent thought that she was pregnant, even though this was ruled out by medical evaluation. An assessment of Lisa's mental status reveals nothing remarkable, and she shows no signs of other psychological disorders (Clark, 1994).

CANNABIS-USE AND CANNABIS-INDUCED DISORDERS

Cannabis dependence and cannabis abuse usually develop over an extended period of time, and those who become dependent typically establish a pattern of chronic use that gradually increases in both frequency and amount. Chronic heavy use is sometimes accompanied by a loss of the pleasurable effects of marijuana and hashish. Although there may also be a corresponding increase in restlessness or anxiety, these symptoms are not seen as frequently as in the chronic use of other substances such as alcohol, cocaine, or amphetamines (drugs used to lift the spirits or control the appetite).

While cannabis-use disorders apply to a person's general level of involvement with marijuana, cannabis-induced disorders describe the intensity of his or her reactions to particular sessions of drug use. Cannabis-induced disorders include cannabis intoxication, cannabis intoxication delirium, cannabis-induced psychotic disorder, and cannabis-induced anxiety disorder. In the case study previously cited, Lisa's symptoms seem to fit the description of cannabis-induced psychotic disorder with hallucinations.

Although most users react to marijuana within minutes, some may not feel much of an effect for several hours. A history of psychological problems, such as conduct disorder or antisocial personality disorder, increases a person's risk for developing cannabis-induced disorders. For a more detailed discussion of the effects of cannabis-use and cannabis-induced disorders, see Chapter 4.

MEDICAL RISKS OF CANNABIS USE

In addition to the psychological complications, which can be quite serious, a number of biological complications can appear with the use of marijuana and hashish. Chronic cannabis use is sometimes associated with weight gain, probably resulting from the overeating and reduced physical activity that often accompany this lifestyle. Another risk is the temporary weakening of a person's immune system, which means that his or her body is less able to fight illness. Also, males may experience reduced testosterone levels.

Cannabis smoke is highly irritating to nasal passages and the throat lining, thus increasing the risk for chronic cough and other bronchial problems. Sinusitis, bronchitis with persistent cough, emphysema, and other lung diseases also can occur with chronic heavy use. Of potentially greater concern, marijuana smoke contains larger amounts of known carcinogens than does tobacco; heavy use may thereby increase the risk of developing various types of cancer.

HOW WIDESPREAD IS CANNABIS USE?

Cannabis is the most widely used illicit psychoactive substance in the United States, not just among adolescents but across all age groups. The

Marijuana and some examples of the paraphernalia used to take the drug: papers used for rolling joints, roach clips for holding the end of a burning marijuana cigarette, and a pipe, called a bong, in which the drug can be smoked. Smoking marijuana is the most popular method of taking the drug in the United States.

USE

most recent survey conducted by NIDA reveals that the use of marijuana and hashish is at its highest level since 1979. The survey reports that about one-half of the population have used marijuana one or more times in their lifetime; 10 percent have used it in the last year; and five percent have used it in the last month.

By charting the use of cannabis over several decades, researchers observe that the risk of drug dependence or drug abuse is generally much greater for young adults than it is for older adults. Also, the level of risk for men is ranked two to three times that for women. These age and gender relationships seem to be attributable to two factors: young adults—and especially young adult males—are historically more likely to take controlled substances, and male users of cannabis are slightly more likely to become dependent on these drugs than are women (Anthony et al., 1995).

As already noted, marijuana and hashish account for most of the nonmedical use of drugs. The findings of one study reveal that 46.3 percent of the population report having used marijuana or hashish at least once as compared with 16.2 percent who have used crack cocaine or cocaine powder and 15.3 percent who have used other psychostimulants, which is the next most frequently used drug group. Researchers have noted that 9.1 percent of cannabis users develop cannabis dependence, as compared to 16.7 percent of cocaine users who develop cocaine dependence and 11.2 percent of all users who become dependent on drugs. At these usage rates, alcohol dependence and cannabis dependence are not the most common substance-abuse syndromes, although they nevertheless occur more frequently than many psychological disorders (Anthony et al., 1995).

USE OF CANNABIS WITH OTHER SUBSTANCES

In addition to the symptoms associated with cannabis use alone, a variety of problems result from the use of cannabis with other substances. Fatal traffic accidents, for example, occur more often in individuals who test positive for cannabis mixed with alcohol and/or other drugs than in the general population.

NIDA notes an increasing number of juveniles who require treatment for regular use and abuse of cannabis. In addition to the resurgence in marijuana use among adolescents, NIDA points to two major factors that may be contributing to the dramatic leap in adverse consequences: (1) higher potency of today's marijuana, and (2) use of marijuana mixed with or in combination with other dangerous drugs.

One mixture combines marijuana with crack cocaine into marijuana cigarettes or blunts. Street names for this combination include "3750s," "diablitos," "primos," "oolies," and "woolies." Joints and blunts are also frequently dipped in PCP (sometimes with formaldehyde and methanol as well) and go by street names such as "happy sticks," "wicky sticks," "illies," "love boat," "wet," or "tical." Both the marijuana-crack and marijuana-PCP combinations are more often found in urban areas, but they have also turned up in some suburbs. In several cities, such as Atlanta and Chicago, teenagers often drink malt liquor when smoking marijuana. Marijuana cigarettes are also sometimes dipped in embalming fluid, as reported in Boston (where they are known as "shermans") and in areas of Texas (NIDA, 1996).

A holy man smokes marijuana in Kathmandu, Nepal. Cannabis has been used in some cultures' religious rites since ancient times.

2
HISTORY OF MARIJUANA
AND HASHISH USE

A ccounts of the use and abuse of alcohol and drugs, including cannabis, are as old as civilization. *Cannabis sativa,* an India hemp plant, was known to have been used for medicinal purposes in China as far back as the third century B.C. Use of cannabis in early Hindu religious rites goes back more than 3,000 years. An urn containing marijuana dating back to 500 B.C. was found in Germany, indicating that Europe's introduction to the drug most likely came a few centuries after it became common in the East. Many Greek, Roman, and biblical authors also described recreational and ritualistic use of cannabis (Milhorn, 1994).

In the Americas, the use of plant stimulants and hallucinogens by Native American tribes has been connected to cultural, religious, and medical ceremonies (Frances and Franklin, 1994). In 1545, Spanish explorers introduced the hemp plant to South America, and in the early 1600s settlers in Virginia began cultivating the plant for making rope and cloth (Royce and Scratchley, 1996).

FROM 19TH-CENTURY EUROPE TO
20TH-CENTURY UNITED STATES

In Europe, the practice of smoking hashish attracted some attention in the mid-1800s, but outside of artistic and literary circles few people knew or cared about its use. Starting around 1850 and during the next 60 years, use of marijuana for medicinal purposes became widely accepted in the United States, especially for treating joint pain, convulsive disorders, hysteria, asthma, rheumatism, and labor pains (Milhorn, 1994). During the latter half of the 19th century, cannabis became popular as a recreational drug, and by 1875 "hasheesh houses," places where the drug could be smoked that were modeled

Narcotics agents prepare to burn a cache of illegal marijuana in 1936. Marijuana became a popular recreational drug in the United States during the period after World War I known as the "Roaring Twenties." By the mid-1930s, several states had passed laws regulating the use of marijuana.

after China's opium dens, began to appear throughout the country. The 1914 Harrison Act, which made nonmedical use of narcotic drugs illegal, temporarily decreased the widespread abuse of marijuana, hashish, and other drugs. During Prohibition (1920–1933), however, when the sale and use of alcohol was illegal, marijuana's popularity as a recreational drug soared (Milhorn, 1994).

Public suspicion about the effects of marijuana and hashish grew toward the end of Prohibition, as a growing crime wave led many to associate the drugs with an increase in violence and wild, uninhibited behavior. Opponents of the drug pointed to the historical Assassins— members of a 10th-century Persian religious sect, who maintained power through assassinating rival leaders while allegedly intoxicated with hashish. In fact, the origin of the word "assassin" has been considered for centuries to be "hashashin," in reference to the use of hashish by these political murderers.

By the mid-1930s, several states had enacted regulations to control the use of marijuana, and the Federal Bureau of Narcotics urged Congress to pass similar federal regulations (Moss and Tarter, 1993). Widespread rumors that marijuana caused crazed violence persisted, even though the violence had more to do with the lifestyle of the smokers than the marijuana they were smoking. In 1937, Congress passed the Marijuana Tax Act, which prohibited even the medicinal use of marijuana (Royce and Scratchley, 1996).

Regulatory efforts continued throughout the 1940s and 1950s. During this period, marijuana was used primarily in urban ghettos and by minority subcultures. But by the late 1950s and 1960s, marijuana and hashish use had spread to high school and college campuses (Royce and Scratchley, 1996). The use of drugs in general skyrocketed during the 1960s; at this time America's youth began a period of intensive questioning of conventional values and institutions and exploring of alternative lifestyles. The passage of the Controlled Substance Act of 1970 made possession of marijuana a misdemeanor, and the intent to sell or transfer it a felony (Milhorn, 1994).

RECENT TRENDS

In the 1960s and early 1970s, marijuana use among young people rose dramatically. One of the driving forces behind this increase in drug use was the "counterculture" movement among young adults. These young people pursued a political agenda that included ending the war in Vietnam, battling over civil rights issues, and attacking environmental abuses. These so-called "hippies" commonly proposed the use of marijuana, as well as hallucinogens such as LSD, to enhance experience and "free the mind." In addition, American soldiers serving in Vietnam found that there was an easily accessible supply of marijuana in that country; many continued to use the drug when they returned home.

INDUSTRIAL HEMP: THE DEBATE

At the beginning of June 1996, actor Woody Harrelson planted four hemp seeds in Kentucky as a protest against the state law banning all forms of hemp cultivation. He was promptly arrested by local police. In January 1997, the district court ruled that the state law was unconstitutional because it classifies industrial hemp, which has no value as a psychoactive drug, with marijuana, making the law "defective due to its overbroad application." The higher circuit court upheld the ruling in July of that year, leading Harrelson to proclaim "Independence Day for Kentucky farmers."

Why the furor over industrial hemp? Though it has no use as a drug, because its level of THC is extremely low (0.3 percent or lower, compared to 3 to 10 percent for marijuana), hemp advocates claim it can be used for many other purposes. The fibers can be made into rope, clothing, paper, and insulation materials, and the seeds can be pressed to extract a highly nutritious oil or used in cosmetics, as fuel, or for printing inks. The United States Department of Agriculture has estimated that an acre of hemp could be used to make up to four times as much paper as an acre of forest land, leading many environmentalists to champion hemp as a way to save trees. Hemp seeds are high in essential fatty acids and proteins, nutrients which are rarely found in such complete form in vegetable foods. Hemp plants also require less fertilizer and pesticide than many of the cash crops grown today, thus causing less pollution of the soil and water supply. The plant was a major cash crop in the early days of this country, supporting many small farmers—including George Washington and Thomas Jefferson. Advocates point to these and other benefits as reasons to legalize the production of industrial hemp.

So far, both state governments and the federal government have been reluctant to legalize it. The Drug Enforcement Agency is concerned that legalized cultivation of hemp would provide a perfect cover for growing illegal marijuana, and that this would make it even more difficult to stop traffic in the drug. Hemp proponents claim that the two varieties of cannabis are cultivated so differently that this would not be a problem. In the late 1990s, several states are considering legalization of hemp and commissioning studies to determine the impact of hemp cultivation on their states' economies as well as on anti-drug efforts.

Actor Woody Harrelson plants hemp seeds in June 1996 as a Kentucky law enforcement official looks on. Harrelson, who planted the seeds to protest a state law banning hemp cultivation for industrial purposes, was arrested immediately after this photo was taken. The law was later deemed unconstitutional by the state's district court. Although industrial hemp contains very little THC, it has been banned in many states due to concern that legalized cultivation would provide a cover for growing illegal marijuana.

Marijuana use among adolescents peaked in the late 1970s, then dropped from 51 percent to 42 percent between 1979 and 1983. Possible explanations for this drop include less peer approval or a new focus on the importance of school to getting a good job (Frances and Franklin, 1994).

Since the mid-1980s, cannabis once again has been gradually increasing in popularity, and peak ages for marijuana abuse were and remain during adolescence and early adulthood. In 1962, approximately four million Americans had used an illicit drug at least once, of which marijuana was the most common (Kleber, 1995); by 1979, that number had climbed to more than 50 million people who had used marijuana at least once (Frances and Franklin, 1994). In 1996, almost 80 million Americans acknowledged having used an illicit drug. A 1996 NIDA survey of more than 15,000 American high school seniors revealed that 90 percent acknowledged having used alcohol, and 4 percent reported daily use. Furthermore, 31 percent reported at least one recent episode of heavy drinking (i.e., five or more drinks in a row). In comparison, 45 percent of seniors reported having used marijuana, with 5 percent reporting daily use (Walter, 1995).

In recent decades, advances in communication, technology, and medicine have led to the production of new illegal drugs, with wider distribution and marketing of drugs produced in many parts of the world. New methods for taking age-old drugs have also emerged—such as smoking cocaine in the form of crack instead of the traditional snorting of powder. And with increasing acceptance, copies of plant-derived psychoactive drugs are being designed in the laboratory for widespread medicinal use (Frances and Franklin, 1994).

Despite having been declared illegal for any purpose six decades ago, cannabis is once again being used as it has been for thousands of years: alleviating health problems. A few of its medicinal uses include relieving nausea from cancer chemotherapy, reducing eye pressure from glaucoma, and improving treatments of epilepsy, multiple sclerosis, AIDS, chronic pain, and migraines, as well as depression and other mood disorders. Using cannabis for these life-easing purposes has not been without controversy, however; citizens and professional groups on both sides of the issue continue to lobby government agencies and Congress regarding the legalization of marijuana.

As for recreational use, many teenagers continue to consider marijuana to be a rite of passage to adulthood, and drug use by adolescents in school continues to rise. Recorded estimates don't even account for those who may be at highest risk for using drugs: the 15 to 20 percent of adolescents who are not enrolled in school. Compounding the concern over this trend are the facts that the marijuana available today is much more potent than it was two decades ago, and that it is believed by some to be a stepping stone to such harder drugs as cocaine, heroin, and PCP (Walter, 1995).

Children with close ties to their families and communities are less likely to use marijuana and other drugs.

3

WHY DO ADOLESCENTS USE DRUGS?

Not all adolescents who use drugs become addicted to them. Some experiment with marijuana but don't like it, thus decreasing the odds that they'll even try other illicit drugs. Some use drugs, though not addictively, for years and eventually stop. Then there are those who become hopelessly addicted, developing destructive drug-use patterns over a period of months or years.

So, why do they do it? There are various possible explanations. For many young people, smoking marijuana may appear to be a direct path to the "in" crowd at school. They think if they use hashish, others will think they are "cool." Or they may believe that smoking marijuana and hashish will make them organized and independent, instead of the reverse. What typically underlies a young person's motivation to try marijuana or hashish, however, is his or her desire to cover up or somehow handle personal uncertainty, even fear, about growing up and becoming an autonomous being. Adolescents who view their parents as oppressive, particularly to the point of feeling imprisoned by them, may find the numbness of a cannabis "high" irresistibly liberating (Kay, 1996).

Adolescents with psychological problems may be drawn to using marijuana and hashish in their desire to rationalize their problems. They would prefer to attribute their strange thoughts and feelings to the drug rather than to their own psychological condition. The culture of "potheads" and "druggies" is more tolerant of psychologically impaired persons than is conventional society. For example, an obsessive-compulsive teen might find warmth and understanding in a group of "Deadheads" (followers of the music group the Grateful Dead), who tend to use drugs, but be considered bizarre by teens seeking acceptance through more traditional activities such as sports, social

Peer pressure tends to have a strong influence on adolescent behavior. Teenagers can be induced to try drugs through direct pressure from friends or indirectly by the impression that "everyone who's cool" does drugs.

clubs, and high school activities (Beeder and Millman, 1995).

So what distinguishes those who abuse drugs from those who don't? Whereas numerous theories about the causes of drug abuse exist, most clinicians agree that no single factor can be blamed for it. Rather, drug abuse is considered to be the result of a number of influences—including biological, psychological, social, and environmental conditions—that interact and affect each individual's likelihood of addiction (Cattarello et al., 1995).

RISK FACTORS

Adolescents who experiment with and later abuse drugs tend to be heavily influenced by a variety of risk factors. They are more often male than female and usually hang around with friends who use drugs. Adolescents who regularly use drugs tend to harbor unconventional beliefs and attitudes and are often hyperactive and sensation seeking.

They typically perform below average in school, in part due to frequent absences, and overall tend to have low educational aspirations.

Some teens who use drugs may feel that their parents don't love them enough; others may not feel very attached to their parents. It's not unusual for adolescent drug users to receive little parental supervision and inconsistent discipline, or to have parents who use alcohol or other drugs themselves. Compared to nonusers, they tend to have very little involvement in a religious community and often reside in troubled neighborhoods. They may suffer from depression or emotional distress (Cattarello et al., 1995).

There are many people who have to deal with a number of these risk factors yet never turn to drugs. It has been observed, however, that the greater the exposure to negative influences, the greater the probability an individual will use (and likely abuse) drugs. For example, one study reveals that 94 percent of the adolescents sampled who had experienced seven or more of the risk factors had used marijuana at least once, whereas only 22 percent of those who had none of the risk factors had tried the drug. Furthermore, although only one percent of those who had no risk factors used marijuana heavily (defined as use at least once a day), 56 percent of those who had seven or more risk factors engaged in heavy use (Cattarello et al., 1995).

There are a number of pathways by which adolescents become involved in drug use, and no single risk factor is sufficient to explain all instances of use. In urban areas where these high-risk factors are more prevalent, youths as young as eight years old may take drugs. Children and adolescents who are not well supervised and have drug-using peers appear to be the most susceptible. In one study of such youngsters, 22 percent started to use marijuana, cocaine, and/or inhalant drugs during the course of the study. Conversely, the same study showed that closely monitored children with very few drug-using friends were an exceptionally low-risk group (Chilcoat and Anthony, 1996).

Although tallying the number of risk factors is helpful in identifying adolescents at high risk for drug use or abuse, it is important to understand that certain factors carry more weight than others at different stages in an individual's life. Generally, those factors that appear to have the greatest influence over an adolescent's choice to use drugs are parental and familial attachment, commitment to and achievement in school, conventionality of beliefs and attitudes, and whether or not their peers use drugs.

Parental attitudes toward drug use often influence the decisions their children make concerning drugs and alcohol. The children of parents who use psychoactive drugs (even legal ones such as tobacco, alcohol, and prescription tranquilizers) may follow their parents' example and use drugs to relieve anxiety and stress.

PARENTAL ATTITUDES

The way parents view and behave toward legal and illegal drug use can heavily influence an adolescent's decision to experiment with drugs. If parents smoke cigarettes and drink alcohol regularly, then their children are likely to view these substances, and perhaps drugs in general, as attractive. One study of 1,222 young adults first contacted in high school found that progression to near-daily use of marijuana was closely associated with having a father who was a heavy drinker or an alcoholic (Cattarello et al., 1995).

An adolescent's propensity to try illicit drugs such as marijuana or cocaine has also been closely linked to parental use of medically prescribed tranquilizers. One possibility is that through their use of such prescription drugs, parents may set the example that drugs can be used to solve psychological problems. Their children, in turn, may then use illicit drugs to handle their own psychological distress. Such an influence suggests that, for some teens, the use of illicit drugs may represent a form of self-medication (Kandel and Davies, 1996).

PEER INFLUENCE

When children are young, direct and consistent parental supervision is important and usually effective; however, as children grow into adolescents, the relative power of parents to influence their behavior tends to diminish, and this power shifts increasingly to peer groups. In fact, friends or peers tend to have as strong an influence as parents on adolescents and teens. Numerous studies have found that peer drug use and time spent with friends can significantly predict whether an individual moves from non-use or light use of alcohol and marijuana to heavier use (Cattarello et al., 1995).

Sixty-five percent of the respondents in one survey attributed their initiation to alcohol and drugs to peer influence. More than half of the respondents surveyed were first given alcohol or drugs directly by a friend. Youths can be influenced by peers either directly, through "peer pressure," or indirectly by the pervading attitude that alcohol and drug use are "cool," and "everyone else does it." Peer pressure is particularly effective at this stage in life, when an adolescent's emotions are on a roller-coaster ride from low self-esteem or depression to feelings of near invincibility.

CURIOSITY

Adolescence is also a time when individuals are trying to break out of childhood and assert themselves as independent and in control. Such growth means greater exploration and sensation seeking, as reflected in the more than 20 percent of respondents to one survey who identified curiosity and fun as reasons for their first use (Dupre et al., 1995).

PREEXISTING PSYCHOLOGICAL PROBLEMS

For some adolescents, there is also an indication that their desire to try drugs is in response to something more serious than usual teenage turbulence. Their rebelliousness, depression, poor school performance, and self-destructive acts may be a sign of underlying disturbance. Some

The environment in which children are raised may have an effect on whether or not they will eventually experiment with marijuana and other drugs. Risk factors for marijuana use, such as availability, peer pressure, and lack of parental supervision, tend to be more prevalent in urban areas—the "inner cities"—than in suburbs. However, suburban youths are also at risk for drug experimentation.

adolescents may use marijuana to avoid handling conflict in their personal and family life. Unfortunately, using marijuana only leads to further breakdown in communications with family, and usually results in changing from nonusing friends to peers who share their interest in drug use (Frances and Franklin, 1994).

CASE STUDY: JOEL

The following vignette illustrates the potential for chronic use of marijuana or hashish to ultimately bring a preexisting condition to the surface. In this case, an adolescent male was diagnosed with cannabis-induced psychotic disorder with delusions, which later revealed the emergence of an underlying schizophrenia:

Joel, who is 16 years old, has been referred to a drug treatment center by his mother, who cited his stealing, poor personal hygiene, school problems, and excessive smoking of marijuana. The problems had developed during the preceding year and were getting worse. Joel is the youngest of three children. He is estranged from his father, who is disabled by heart disease and reportedly has a drinking problem. Joel has recently begun to withdraw from his mother and steal from her and his sister. He has also begun to refuse to bathe and use deodorant, causing his friends to withdraw from him. During the previous school year, he threw tantrums and walked out of class, resulting in his expulsion and failing a grade.

Joel admits to smoking an average of one or two joints a day, and having begun to smoke when he was 11 years old. He denies using other drugs except an occasional drink of alcohol. He denies experiencing hallucinations or paranoid thoughts. Although he denies having sleep problems, his mother reports that he stays up late at night and cooks at odd hours, sometimes burning food and utensils. Joel stutters and expresses a concern that his stuttering could be connected with his having caught a fishhook in his hand when he was five.

An assessment of Joel's mental status reveals a somewhat dull and slow mental ability and a noticeable stutter. He has some difficulty concentrating, and his thinking is inconsistent. When asked about his behavior, he states that it has been determined by his astrological sign (Clark, 1994).

It is difficult to determine if a marijuana-smoking adolescent suffered from psychological problems before beginning to use the drug, as the drug use masks the usual symptoms. It is clear, however, that such preexisting problems create a greater danger from the drug abuse and delay critical treatment of the underlying psychological disorder. In most cases, only after the adolescent is drug free can he or she begin to focus on other issues of mental health (Cattarello et al., 1995).

MOVING FROM USE TO ABUSE

A number of studies of drug use progression found that teenage use of liquor and cigarettes is associated with the highest rates of future marijuana abuse. Drinking alcohol seems to be a stronger predictor of later marijuana use than smoking tobacco. Thereafter, marijuana may be a key stepping-stone to other illicit drugs, and the frequency of marijuana use is directly linked to the level of later use of more serious drugs (Frances and Franklin, 1994).

A more recent problem is that adolescents are increasingly going straight to cocaine use without prolonged experimentation with marijuana. This may be because their initial experiences with marijuana may not have produced significant adverse effects, so they may be less fearful of trying other drugs. Thus, an indirect danger of marijuana is that it introduces youth to the drug culture and lowers their inhibitions about using harder drugs (Frances and Franklin, 1994).

It is important to note, however, that the factors that constitute risk for drug use do not in themselves predict whether or not a person will inevitably move from recreational use to abuse. In general, the use of drugs appears to be more a function of social and peer factors, whereas addiction to drugs seems more directly connected to genetics and psychological health. Whatever the risks, the chances of an adolescent's progressing from single drug or alcohol use to more severe forms of multiple drug and alcohol addiction can be reduced by a number of counteracting positive influences (Cattarello et al., 1995).

PROTECTIVE FACTORS

Why do some adolescents not use drugs? In addition to the risk factors already cited, adolescent drug use is influenced by protective factors. For example, a boy may have friends who use drugs, and he may not be doing very well in school—two risk factors—but he may also have such protective factors as high self-esteem and commitment to religious faith. These protective factors interact with accompanying risks to increase or decrease the odds of an adolescent becoming addicted to drugs (Cattarello et al., 1995).

Protective factors vary in strength depending on the adolescent. Individual personality and character, living conditions, and environment can mean the difference between healthy resilience and shaky vulnerability to dangerous drug use. Specific protective factors include having a close relationship with parents and family members, as well as having parents who do not have a drinking or drug problem. Interestingly, being female seems to reduce the risk of drug abuse, as girls are less likely than boys to use drugs in the first place. High academic achievement, commitment to school, and educational aspirations give teens more constructive ways to spend their time. High socioeconomic status may contribute as well. Adolescents who have a strong faith in religion and nurture close supportive relationships with peers and others outside the family also are more likely to resist abusing drugs. In terms of individual characteristics, high self-esteem and independence, creativity, and a calm or relaxed temperament are crucial protective factors (Cattarello et al., 1995).

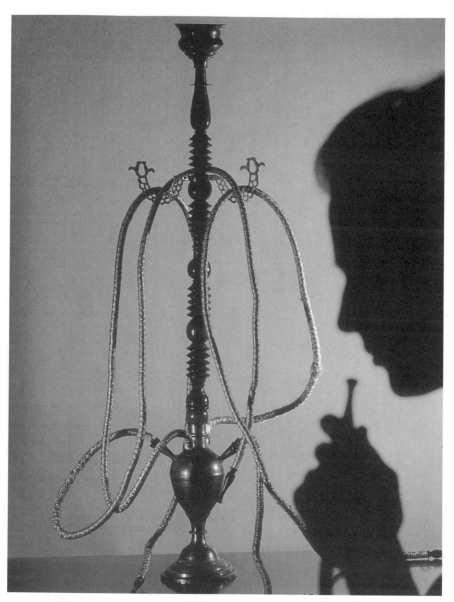

Some users smoke marijuana to escape from the pressures of daily life. Users who are psychologically dependent on marijuana may believe that they need the drug to "unwind" after a hectic day. This man is using a water pipe to smoke the drug.

4

HOW ARE USERS AFFECTED?

In most areas of their lives, students who regularly use drugs perform at a lower level than peers who are nonusers. In the early stages of drug use, usually as students move from alcohol and cigarettes to experimentation with marijuana, they tend to distance themselves from schoolwork and extracurricular activities. Eventually, these teens are likely to grow more detached from their parents and home life, especially those who progress from marijuana to cocaine or other illicit drugs. Throughout the entire progression from alcohol to marijuana to harder drugs, one effect is constant: the person's overall health, both physical and psychological, is sure to deteriorate.

For many young people, experimentation with cannabis or other drugs may be short-lived and have no serious social, psychological, or medical repercussions. In other cases, drug use may become a dangerously large part of their lives, possibly leading to such destructive drug-taking patterns as abuse or dependence.

Each individual user can experience unique psychological symptoms, depending on the dose, the method of administration, the personality of the user, previous experience with the drug, and personal expectations. Inexperienced and first-time users may not experience a marked high, even if they inhale adequately. Over time, marijuana users may become more sensitive to the subtle psychoactive effects most associated with intoxication. Chronic users may even learn to suppress undesirable feelings and behaviors with long-term exposure (Frances and Franklin, 1994).

SHORT-TERM EFFECTS OF
MARIJUANA AND HASHISH

The interaction of drug and setting appears to have a considerable influence on the short-term effects of cannabis. Users typically feel a peak high within 10 to 30 minutes of smoking a joint that has a significant level of THC.

The high usually lasts from two to four hours, depending on the dose; however, behavioral, psychological, and physical impairment may continue several hours longer. If ingested orally, cannabis tends to take from 45 minutes to several hours to affect the user, and it does so with more powerful psychoactive effects. Effects usually last three to four hours, lasting somewhat longer and having more intensity than when the cannabis is smoked. Physical signs of a person who is high include red eyes, dilated pupils, rapidly beating heart, dry mouth, and coughing (Frances and Franklin, 1994). The magnitude of the behavioral and physiological changes depends on the dose and the method of administration, as well as on the individual characteristics of the person using the substance—including rate of absorption, tolerance, and sensitivity to the effects of the substance.

A marijuana or hashish high can cause users to feel detached. Time seems to pass more slowly, although users tend to feel no sense of boredom and little need for activity. They often experience increased appetite and thirst and have a keener sense of color, sound, pattern, texture, and taste. Mood changes vary profoundly, and a mild euphoria is not uncommon. Some individuals, however, may feel anxious and depressed, inaccurately perceiving problems as either more or less pressing. They tend to become much more introspective, often philosophical, and have an increased ability to be absorbed in sensual experiences. Some users may feel an increased level of self-confidence, occasionally nearing delusions of invincibility (Beeder and Millman, 1995). Other users undergo bouts of drowsiness or hyperactivity and have intermittent fits of unprovoked laughter. In a disconnected manner, ideas may flow rapidly and be altered in importance. There may be phases of extreme relaxation and feeling like one is floating. Some experience heightened sexual desire, as well as physical illusions and hallucinations (Frances and Franklin, 1994).

LONG-TERM EFFECTS

Over time, continued use of marijuana and hashish often results in a decrease in the pleasurable effects experienced during a high. Conversely, many undesirable effects tend to persist, although some studies have found that the usual speeding heart rate, dry mouth, and lightheadedness tend to lessen after a while. Numerous studies have demonstrated that marijuana intoxication impairs automobile driving, airplane flying, and other complex skilled activities because of impaired attention span,

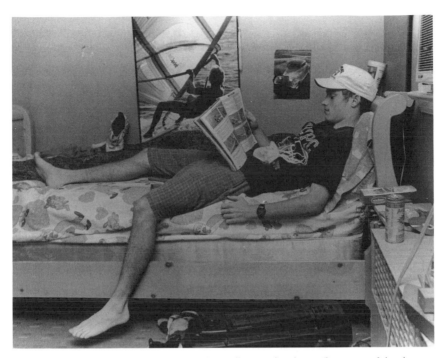

A high may last from two to four hours depending on the size and potency of the dose. Although time may seem to pass slowly, users generally do not feel bored and may be content with little activity.

physical coordination, and depth perception for up to 10 hours or more after use (Frances and Franklin, 1994).

In school, the workplace, or any situation in which clarity of mind is required, marijuana may have detrimental effects. Even after the strongest intoxication effects recede, a morning hangover may interfere with functioning. Ability to speak coherently, form concepts, concentrate, and transfer information from immediate to long-term memory is impaired. For some users, milder symptoms of anxiety, confusion, fear, and increased dependency on the drug can progress to panic, paranoia, and depression. Higher doses of delta-9-THC will correspondingly increase the chance of toxic reactions (Frances and Franklin, 1994).

PSYCHOLOGICAL CONDITIONS ASSOCIATED WITH MARIJUANA AND HASHISH USE

The American Psychiatric Association (APA) classifies the effects of marijuana and hashish into cannabis-use disorders and cannabis-induced disorders. The former include cannabis dependence and abuse; the latter include cannabis intoxication, cannabis intoxication delirium, cannabis-induced psychotic disorder, and cannabis-induced anxiety disorder. Additional complications include flashback syndrome, chronic cannabis/amotivational syndrome, and cannabis withdrawal.

Although these reactions range from relatively mild to severe in their long-term effects on cannabis users, it should be noted that there is little evidence that marijuana or hashish causes permanent changes in the central nervous system or in behavior. Unlike harder drugs such as heroin or cocaine, cannabis use is usually not life-threatening, although there are still some serious risks. Individuals with underlying cardiovascular disease, for example, could suffer serious damage from the increased heart rate and blood pressure that occur with marijuana use. All users could suffer from marijuana's potential suppression of the immune system. And perhaps more serious for frequent users, cannabis smoke contains carcinogens similar to those in tobacco smoke, and chronic heavy marijuana use can lead to lung disease (Frances and Franklin, 1994).

CANNABIS-USE DISORDERS

Users who experience any psychological or physical problems in association with cannabis may suffer from cannabis abuse or dependence. In addition to their interference with everyday life, cannabis-use disorders have been linked to certain psychiatric disorders among adolescents—including mood, conduct, antisocial personality, attention-deficit/hyperactivity, eating, and anxiety disorders. However, considerable research is still needed to understand fully the interaction between marijuana and such disorders. The most common psychiatric disorders identified in substance-abusing adolescents are mood disorders among females and conduct disorders among males (Walter, 1995).

CANNABIS DEPENDENCE

According to the APA, the usual signs that a person suffers from cannabis dependence include having all-consuming thoughts about, and exhibiting actions that focus on, getting and using cannabis; impaired physical performance; and difficulty functioning at work and in social situations (Beeder and Millman, 1995). Such individuals may use very potent cannabis throughout the day over a period of months or years, and they may spend several hours a day seeking a dealer and using the substance. They use marijuana or hashish compulsively, and,

Marijuana use tends to negatively impact classroom performance. Drug intoxication impairs a person's ability to concentrate, speak coherently, and transfer information from immediate to long-term memory. These debilitating effects may persist once the high has receded.

although they do not generally develop a physiological dependence, some who use cannabis chronically may develop a tolerance to most of the effects.

CANNABIS ABUSE

Cannabis abuse is distinguished from cannabis dependence by a higher level of tolerance and the greater likelihood of psychological or physical problems associated with the more frequent use of marijuana and hashish. Considered more severe and destructive than dependence, cannabis abuse is seen in individuals who repeatedly get high on marijuana or hashish. Marijuana abuse usually entails daily use, large amounts of the substance, and problematic behavior. As cannabis abusers frequently try to buy and usually carry the drugs, legal problems can result from arrests for cannabis solicitation and possession.

A 10-year-old boy smokes marijuana in New York City's East Village. In urban areas, children as young as eight years old may take drugs, particularly if parental supervision is lacking and they have peers who use drugs.

CANNABIS-INDUCED DISORDERS

Cannabis dependence and cannabis abuse can be regarded as umbrella terms that reflect how pervasive the use of marijuana and hashish is in a user's life. Under those umbrellas are cannabis-induced disorders that define the more immediate effects of getting high. For example, someone who is cannabis dependent may smoke marijuana one day and experience cannabis intoxication; that same person may go on to use cannabis more regularly and, after a particular episode of getting "high," may suffer the symptoms of cannabis-induced psychotic disorder.

Several studies suggest that high doses and prolonged use of cannabis can lead to prolonged or chronic psychotic disorders. In most cases the psychotic symptoms lessen after days or weeks; in other cases the symptoms are chronic or permanent. Psychological problems associated with chronic marijuana use depend on the user's pre-drug psychological condition and how it is affected by the drug. In other words, the user's condition may be the result of marijuana use or dependence or, conversely, it can be the cause of a drug-use pattern (Beeder and Millman, 1995).

CANNABIS INTOXICATION

Persons who suffer from cannabis intoxication show significant difficulty adapting to or functioning in everyday situations, as well as psychological changes during or shortly after use of marijuana or hashish. As already noted, intoxication typically begins with a high feeling, followed by symptoms that include euphoria with random, inappropriate laughter, sedate and lethargic behavior, and weakened short-term memory. Intoxicated individuals also tend to have difficulty carrying out complex mental processes and have impaired judgment, distorted sensory perceptions, impaired movement, and the sensation that time is passing slowly. Occasionally, a person can feel anxiety (which can be severe), restlessness, or social withdrawal.

CANNABIS INTOXICATION DELIRIUM

As the name implies, cannabis intoxication delirium is more severe than cannabis intoxication and magnifies a similar set of symptoms. Disturbances from frequent cannabis intoxication develop over a short period of time (usually hours to days) and tend to fluctuate during the course of the day. Using marijuana or hashish on a regular basis can cause individuals to experience their surroundings with less clarity and awareness and have difficulty focusing, sustaining, or shifting their attention. They tend to have problems with memory and speech and be disoriented. They may even hallucinate, although this is rare except when very high blood levels of THC are reached.

A toxic delirium occurs most often after a person ingests or smokes a large amount of marijuana or hashish. This condition is marked by clouded consciousness, confusion, impaired thinking, and physical imbalance. Users may experience impaired memory, visual and auditory hallucinations, paranoia, and violent or bizarre behavior. Their speech may become disconnected, and involuntary eye movement is not uncommon. The syndrome typically lasts from a few hours to a few days (Beeder and Millman, 1995).

CANNABIS-INDUCED PSYCHOTIC DISORDER

Cannabis-induced psychotic disorder is defined by the APA as the presence of prominent delusions or hallucinations that are a direct physiological effect of cannabis use. Individuals with this disorder may develop delusions within a couple of hours of smoking marijuana or hashish. For example, a person who develops cannabis-induced psychotic disorder may believe that he or she is being attacked or persecuted, or that he or she is the greatest, most powerful person in the world. At the same time, people with this disorder don't tend to suffer clouding of consciousness or significant loss of intellectual abilities. Users may temporarily lose touch with reality, feel emotionally unstable and confused, and suffer extreme anxiety, sometimes to the point of paranoia. These experiences can sometimes cause violent behavior. Visual and auditory hallucinations are unusual, but they do occur. Following such episodes, it is not uncommon for the user to forget about his or her behavior. The disorder usually remits within a day but in some cases may persist for several days (Beeder and Millman, 1995).

The following case shows a direct relationship between use of marijuana and the onset of delusional thinking, or cannabis-induced psychotic disorder with delusions. In this young woman's case, marijuana use also may have triggered a delayed post-traumatic stress disorder due to the death of her uncle (Clark, 1994):

Susan is 15 years old and was referred to a mental health clinic from a crisis center where she had been evaluated two months earlier because she was having crying spells and hallucinations. She is accompanied by her mother, who said that Susan has been having trouble sleeping since the death of an uncle 18 months ago. Susan had been fairly close to her uncle and was the person who discovered him dead. Both Susan and her mother indicate that Susan had been fine before the death and had shown no previous signs of emotional or behavioral problems.

Susan reported that she had gone to the crisis center because of a "paranoid" sensation that hands were grabbing at her and her insides were being pulled out after having smoked two joints with a friend. She became hysterical, crying and screaming. She was taken to the hospital but was not medicated. When her symptoms persisted for another day, she was taken back to the emergency room, from which she was referred to the crisis center.

Susan has smoked marijuana since the age of 13. She shared up to seven or eight joints at a time with several other people, never smoked alone, and smoked only on weekends. She had no prior or subsequent bad experiences with marijuana and denied use of other drugs, except an occasional beer. Susan suffers from disturbing dreams involving

Amotivational syndrome may be exhibited by those who chronically use high doses of marijuana or hashish. Symptoms include apathy, passivity, decreased capacity to carry out long-term plans, poor judgement, and fatigue.

death and is still uncomfortable about going into the basement of her home, where she had discovered her uncle's body. Although an assessment of her mental status reveals depression and an impaired ability to concentrate, the only signs of psychological problems are the delusions she experienced after smoking marijuana (Clark, 1994).

Cannabis-induced psychotic disorder appears to be rare, although chronic use may sustain the psychotic state (McGlashan and Krystal, 1995). In fact, many clinicians question whether such a reaction from cannabis use alone can occur. Despite the high prevalence of marijuana use in the West, cannabis psychosis is much more commonly reported in Asian cultures, perhaps because oral ingestion of cannabis is more

Those who use marijuana frequently may experience effects similar to hallucinogen-induced "bad trips." These range from mild levels of anxiety to paranoia, delusions, hallucinations, and severe anxiety resembling a panic attack.

common in Asia than in the West. Oral administration of cannabis results in a pattern and concentration of cannabinoids within the user's system that is different from the concentration that occurs from smoking (Moss and Tarter, 1993).

Cannabis-induced psychosis is sometimes caused by the presence of other chemicals that have been mixed with the marijuana or hashish. At one time it was quite common to lace joints with phencyclidine (PCP), or "angel dust"—which by itself can produce many of the symptoms associated with cannabis-induced psychosis (McGlashan and Krystal, 1995). A more recent, highly toxic street mixture goes by the name of "illy." It consists of cannabis and variable amounts of formaldehyde, methanol, and PCP. The effects of this combination typically vary from disorientation, confusion, and loss of recent memory to violent, out-of-control behavior and bizarre speech, lasting hours or days. A more severe state is toxic psychosis, represented by hallucinations, delusions, and bizarre and disorganized behavior. The most serious cases have resulted in catatonia—in which a person becomes schizophrenic, alternating between mental stupor, confusion, and intense excitement—and coma lasting several hours (McGlashan and Krystal, 1995).

CANNABIS-INDUCED ANXIETY DISORDER

The most frequently reported adverse reactions to cannabis are anxiety reactions and panic attacks. Obsessions or compulsions can also occur with these disorders. These generally occur during the period of intoxication and usually abate within minutes or hours. Anxiety reactions are more likely to occur in users who have little or no experience with taking the drug, who are unfamiliar with the drug's effects, and who take it in an unfamiliar setting. These reactions vary in intensity and range from mild discomfort to panic (Beeder and Millman, 1995).

The APA points out, however, that some of these symptoms can be caused by a preexisting anxiety disorder. This is particularly true if the symptoms precede the use of marijuana or hashish; persist for a substantial period of time (for example, about a month) after severe intoxication; or are excessive given the amount of cannabis used.

FLASHBACK SYNDROME

Prolonged use of marijuana or hashish can cause flashbacks, which are defined as psychotic experiences from past psychedelic or marijuana experiences (Frances and Franklin, 1994). A flashback is a seemingly realistic recurrence of feelings and perceptions originally experienced under the influence of cannabis (or a psychedelic drug). Most flashbacks are episodes of visual distortion, reexperienced intense emotion, or physical symptoms. Flashbacks generally decrease in number and intensity over time, but in rare cases they become more frequent (Beeder and Millman, 1995).

CHRONIC CANNABIS /AMOTIVATIONAL SYNDROME

An amotivational syndrome has been described in various parts of the world in persons who chronically use high doses of marijuana or hashish. Many of the studies were conducted in Jamaica, India, and Egypt (Frances and Franklin, 1994). Chronic users exhibit apathy, a diminished capacity to carry out long-term plans, an inability to master new problems, and a deterioration of personal hygiene. These users are described as withdrawn, passive, easily distracted, and having poor judgment. Generally, chronic cannabis use leads to impaired memory

Marijuana use may lead to aggressive, violent behavior and conduct disorder. Conduct disorder includes repeated violation of social rules and others' personal rights and can result in delinquency and social problems.

and fatigue, producing a "fog" that lasts several weeks after quitting cannabis use.

Although there is skepticism about the existence of this syndrome, it is clear that heavy cannabis use, by adolescents in particular, tends to stifle ambition and drive and impair school performance. However, some individuals have shown enthusiasm in the pursuit of one particular goal, such as intense involvement with rock or reggae music. In general, chronic heavy cannabis use has been associated with profound changes in perspective, dress, and behavior (Beeder and Millman, 1995).

CANNABIS WITHDRAWAL

Some heavy users of marijuana and hashish who have attempted to quit have experienced irritable or anxious moods accompanied by tremors, marked perspiration, nausea, loss of appetite, and sleep disturbance (Frances and Franklin, 1994). Controversy exists over whether such withdrawal symptoms are clinically significant or if they greatly contribute to the persistent use of cannabis. However, there is increasing recognition of the fact that some adolescent chronic cannabis users may find it difficult to quit—some due to their intense desire for an altered state of consciousness, others because of their fear of unpleasant withdrawal symptoms (Duffy and Milin, 1996).

The following case study illustrates withdrawal symptoms described in an adolescent with a history of chronic heavy cannabis use. She came to a treatment center seeking medical advice regarding the symptoms:

Mary, a 17-year-old with a history of bulimia nervosa, reports having smoked one gram of cannabis daily since age 15, increasing to two to three grams daily approximately six months prior to visiting the treatment center. Mary is diagnosed with cannabis dependence and has a history of cocaine and alcohol use, although she does not use either regularly or heavily.

Prior to her assessment she had attempted to reduce her use of cannabis on several occasions; however, withdrawal symptoms, which would occur within 24 hours, led her back to the drug, usually by the fourth day. These symptoms are flu-like and include irritable and unstable moods and drug cravings. Her longest drug-free period was seven days, during which she experienced the above-mentioned withdrawal symptoms as well as additional marked perspiration, shakiness, chills, fluctuations in appetite, and initial insomnia. Mary resumed cannabis use by the seventh day because of the intolerable discomfort associated with the withdrawal symptoms. She then increased her daily usage to four to six grams. Now, after several months of outpatient motivational therapy and a young-adult inpatient chemical dependency program, Mary successfully quit using marijuana (Duffy and Milin, 1996).

In Mary's case, it was the unpleasant withdrawal symptoms rather than the psychological drug cravings that led her to return to smoking marijuana. Her experience illustrates some of the disturbing symptoms frequent users can experience when they try to quit (Duffy and Milin, 1996).

OTHER RELATED DISORDERS

In addition to the psychological problems listed above, a person who

MARIJUANA AND PREGNANCY

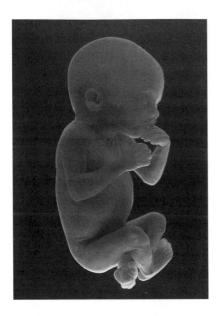

It is unclear whether or not marijuana use has a negative impact on the developing fetus. Studies have shown that heavy marijuana use, especially during the early months of a pregnancy, may increase the risk of certain birth defects as well as low birth weight. More research needs to be done to determine the effects of marijuana on fetuses.

Several drugs, including alcohol and tobacco, have been shown to cause complications during pregnancy and birth and to lead to below-average birth weight in babies. Marijuana is one of the most studied drugs, but researchers are divided on whether use of the drug has a negative effect on pregnancy.

The Ottawa Prenatal Prospective Study reported that heavy marijuana use during pregnancy (five or more marijuana cigarettes per week) resulted in a shorter

uses marijuana is at risk for other disorders, such as mood disorders, disruptive behavior disorders, eating disorders, and anxiety disorders. These disorders, as classified by the APA in the *Diagnostic and Statistical Manual of Mental Illness (DSM-IV)*, are listed below:

MOOD DISORDERS

Mood disorders are psychological disturbances characterized by extreme mood swings. The two types of mood disorders are unipolar (depressive) disorders and bipolar (manic depressive) disorders. Unipolar disorders are indicated by periods of severe depression, typically last-

gestation period for the fetus. The study also noted that the risk of two types of birth defects was increased in these children. One, ocular hypertelorism, is characterized by an abnormally wide spacing of the eyes and slight mental retardation. The other, epicanthus, is a defect of the eyelid that is characterized by an extra fold of skin.

A 1986 study performed at Johns Hopkins school of Medicine found that infants born to women who smoked more than two marijuana cigarettes per week during their pregnancy were less responsive to stimuli, easier to startle, and more likely to suffer tremors. These are signs that these children's nervous systems were not as well developed as those of other newborn children whose mothers did not smoke the drug. However, this study also found that a month later these characteristics were no longer apparent, indicating that these children's neurological development had accelerated. A study by psycholosist Ernest C. Abel indicated that significantly smaller babies were born to women who smoked three or more joints per day during their first three months of pregnancy. Low birth weight has been linked to many developmental problems in children.

Some research indicated that women who used marijuana during their pregnancy gained more weight than those who did not. This could be considered a positive sign, a indicator of a successful pregnancy and healthy birth. In addition, other researchers argue that factors other than marijuana use cause birth defects and low birth weight in pregnancy, such as use of alcohol or other drugs, and malnutrition. Until these questions are answered definitively, research on the effects of marijuana during pregnancy will continue.

ing more than two weeks and causing the sufferer to lose interest in activities, feel irritated or sad all the time, feel worthless or guilty, have difficulty concentrating, change sleeping and eating patterns, lose energy, and/or consider or even attempt suicide. Bipolar disorders include depressive episodes, but they also include manic episodes or episodes that show both manic and depressive characteristics (called mixed episodes). In manic episodes, people feel extremely energized for an extended period of time, often showing signs of inflated self-esteem, decreased need for sleep, increased risk-taking, distractibility, and irritability. There are several different bipolar disorders, showing different combinations of depressive, manic, hypomanic (a less intense, less long-lasting manic episode), and mixed episodes. Mood disorders are among the most common psychological disorders and can usually be treated with a combination of therapy and medication.

ATTENTION DEFICIT/HYPERACTIVITY DISORDER

Attention deficit/hyperactivity disorder (ADHD) is a developmental disorder that involves self-control and frequently affects children or adolescents. Children with ADHD are often unable to pay attention in school or at home, are impulsive or easily distracted, and have difficulty staying still or doing activities that require long periods of attention or inactivity. Many times, a child with ADHD will also exhibit emotional instability, frequently because of the social difficulties caused by the disorder. Intensity of the symptoms varies among different settings; symptoms may be more evident in the heavily structured environment of the classroom than in the less rigid atmosphere of the home, for example. If a diagnosis of ADHD is reached, the child can normally be treated with stimulant medication such as Ritalin, which gives him or her increased ability to concentrate and focus on tasks.

CONDUCT DISORDER

Conduct disorder, like ADHD, is one of a group of psychological disorders called disruptive behavior disorders. Conduct disorder includes some symptoms that are similar to ADHD, such as impulsivity and inattention. However, conduct disorder also includes more outwardly directed symptoms that involve the repeated violation of social rules or others' personal rights, sometimes including violent behaviors. This disorder begins most often during late childhood or early adolescence and can be the cause of many forms of misbehavior, from deception to armed robbery. The APA has divided conduct disorder into two subtypes: childhood-onset and adolescent-onset. The childhood-onset type, defined as beginning before the child is 10 years old, is considered more severe and more likely to lead to further problems such as delinquency, violence, and disorders such as antisocial personality disorder in adults.

EATING DISORDERS

Eating disorders involve an inability or unwillingness to maintain normal, healthy eating patterns. This can mean that the person refuses to eat enough and/or drastically overexercises (anorexia nervosa), or binge-eats and then rapidly purges the food by vomiting or laxative abuse (bulimia). These disorders, more common in young women than men, can have serious health consequences if they are not detected and treated. Malnutrition can cause anorexic and bulimic patients to develop anemia, heart arrhythmias, calcium deficiencies that may lead to osteoporosis, and, in female patients, the disruption of menstrual cycles and possibly permanent damage to the reproductive system. Bulimics may also suffer from ulcers of the stomach and esophagus caused by excessive vomiting. In severe cases, sufferers from either disorder may die of malnutrition or its complications. It is very difficult for a person with anorexia or bulimia to conquer the disorder without help, but treatment is often successful, especially if the patient is brought to doctors in the early stages of the disorder. Most often, treatment involves individual or group therapy, sometimes combined with medication to help combat the depression that often accompanies eating disorders. In severe cases, a patient must usually be hospitalized for the first part of the treatment to ensure that he or she does not continue to practice destructive eating habits.

ANXIETY DISORDERS

Anxiety disorders are a broad group encompassing such varied problems as obsessive-compulsive disorder, phobias, panic attacks, and post-traumatic stress disorder. The common thread possessed by all of these disorders is the tendency to exhibit excessive fear, nervousness, or anxiety in a situation that should not cause such a severe reaction. Often, these disorders interfere with a person's normal life, since he or she will take steps to try to avoid the situations that cause anxiety. For example, a person with a social phobia may become withdrawn and cease to associate with large groups of people, or a person with obsessive-compulsive disorder may experience an intense fear of having his or her house or room broken into and thus compulsively check all the locks every few minutes. Most of these disorders can be successfully treated with therapy, once the individual realizes that he or she has a problem and wants to try to overcome it.

Homelessness is among the many social problems, including crime, domestic violence, welfare, education, and AIDS, that are affected by substance abuse. In the last 30 years, the number of people using drugs has increased dramatically in the United States; an increase in related societal problems has occurred as a result.

5

THE IMPACT ON SOCIETY

Substance abuse and dependence are major public health problems in the United States. Health care costs related to substance abuse and its associated complications are estimated to be approximately $140 billion (about 15 percent) of our total $900 billion health care budget. But the impact of substance abuse cannot be measured simply by health care funds alone, for it extends to most other social problems we encounter as a nation. In fact, crime, domestic violence, AIDS, homelessness, education, welfare, and an internationally competitive workplace are all affected by our failure to deal adequately with substance abuse and dependence (Kleber, 1995).

Cannabis in particular is associated with a significant number of deaths from suicide, vehicular accidents, other accidents, and homicide. Unfortunately, the extent to which cannabis is involved is not well documented because autopsy reports typically do not identify cannabis as a contributor in cases of violent or uncertain deaths, any more than they would mention traces of nicotine in such cases (Westermeyer, 1992).

PREVALENCE OF DRUG USE AND ABUSE

In the general population, the number of persons addicted to or in trouble with various substances is enormous: more than 50 million people are addicted to tobacco, and 18 million or more have drinking problems. Topping the list of all illicit drugs, marijuana is used at least once a week by more than five million individuals. Other illicit drugs—including cocaine, heroin, LSD, PCP, and ecstasy (MDMA or methylenedioxymethamphetamine)—are used weekly by more than three million. Although these figures reflect adults and adolescents combined, those between the ages of 15 and 24 years show more cases of drug dependence than any other age group (Kleber, 1995).

Use of drugs may lead to theft, vandalism, and other forms of aggression. Juvenile delinquency should be taken seriously and addressed before it leads to more serious consequences.

A PROGRESSION OF BEHAVIOR

Although cannabis is often viewed as a fairly benign substance compared to cocaine or heroin, its use by more than five million persons a week is associated with thousands of users each year going to emergency rooms for problems secondary to marijuana use, as well as numerous cases of abuse and dependence that require psychiatric intervention. And the current resurgence of marijuana use among adolescents and young adults suggests that clinics and hospitals will only see an increase in such cases (Kleber and Galanter, 1995).

One study examines the progression from childhood aggression to adolescent drug use to delinquency over a 20-year period. The findings suggest that drug use patterns cause theft, vandalism, and aggression by reducing inhibitions in the adolescent and young adult. Many adolescents commit crimes for money to purchase drugs, particularly stealing, either from their parents or from strangers. They also associate with and often idolize other drug users, some of whom are also delinquent. Another mediating link between drug use and delinquency is the adolescent's relations with family members. Drug use strains the parent-child relationship, which, in turn, causes the adolescent to turn away from conventional attitudes and pursue delinquent behavior (Brook et al., 1996).

The findings of this study have several implications for society in general. First, it is thought that if childhood aggression can be managed properly and early, there is less danger of later drug use in adolescence and young adulthood. Drug use and delinquency in adolescence should not be taken lightly, since these behaviors tend to progress into adulthood. Finally, efforts to minimize drug use at each stage—childhood, adolescence, and adulthood—are likely to result in a decrease in delinquent behavior (Brook et al., 1996).

CANNABIS AS A "GATEWAY" DRUG

One of the most hotly debated controversies over marijuana use today is the hypothesis that it acts as a "gateway drug"; that is, that marijuana leads to use of other, "harder" drugs such as heroin and cocaine. In 1995, the Partnership for a Drug-Free America, along with NIDA and the White House Office of Drug Control Policy, announced a new campaign against marijuana based on this premise, claiming that reduction of marijuana use would lead to reduction of other drug use. Critics claim that the data used to support this hypothesis are flawed and that for the overwhelming percentage of users, marijuana acts as a "terminus" rather than a "gateway" drug.

One of the major pieces of evidence for the "gateway" effect is a report by the Center on Addiction and Substance Abuse, which uses data from NIDA's 1991 National Household Survey on Drug Abuse to make the claim that marijuana users are 85 percent more likely than non-users to try cocaine. They calculated this figure by dividing the proportion of marijuana users who have used cocaine (17 percent) by the proportion of cocaine users who have never used marijuana (0.2 percent). Critics say that the resulting figure does not reflect the risk factor of marijuana users to try cocaine but rather the percentage of cocaine users who have tried marijuana. Dr. John P. Morgan, a medical doctor who is affiliated with the National Organization for Reform of Marijuana Laws (NORML), wrote of this finding, "The obvious statistic not publicized by CASA is that most marijuana users—83 percent— never use cocaine."

In another study, a team at Scripps Research Institute in California attempted to show that marijuana use conditions the brain to be more receptive to cocaine or heroin addiction. The team used a chemical designed to mimic the effects of marijuana, causing rats to become dependent on it and then analyzing the effects on the rats' brains while they were on the drug and after it had been withdrawn. They found withdrawal symptoms like those of rats in withdrawal from cocaine, heroin, and alcohol, as well as significant neurotransmitter changes in the rats' brain chemistry, which they believe would predispose the rats to be receptive to other drugs. Skeptics point out that the social factors influencing drug use are completely absent from studies done with rats, that the drug used was synthetic rather than marijuana itself, and that very few human marijuana users ever reach a level of dependence on the drug.

Opponents of the "gateway" classification point to Holland's drug policy as an example. Holland's government focuses its drug policy largely on attempts to control any gateway effects. Dutch officials legalized marijuana in certain government-controlled situations several years ago, as part of an attempt to keep young marijuana users out of the illegal markets where they would be exposed to cocaine and heroin. Despite this easy availability, only 13.6 percent of Dutch teenagers surveyed in 1992 had tried marijuana, compared with 38 percent of U.S. teens. Officials admit that this is an increase over 1984's rate of 4.8 per-

sevcre state is toxic psychosis, represented by hallucinations, delusions, and bizarre and disorganized behavior. The most serious cases have resulted in catatonia—in which a person becomes schizophrenic, alternating between mental stupor, confusion, and intense excitement—and coma lasting several hours (McGlashan and Krystal, 1995).

CANNABIS-INDUCED ANXIETY DISORDER

The most frequently reported adverse reactions to cannabis are anxiety reactions and panic attacks. Obsessions or compulsions can also occur with these disorders. These generally occur during the period of intoxication and usually abate within minutes or hours. Anxiety reactions are more likely to occur in users who have little or no experience with taking the drug, who are unfamiliar with the drug's effects, and who take it in an unfamiliar setting. These reactions vary in intensity and range from mild discomfort to panic (Beeder and Millman, 1995).

The APA points out, however, that some of these symptoms can be caused by a preexisting anxiety disorder. This is particularly true if the symptoms precede the use of marijuana or hashish; persist for a substantial period of time (for example, about a month) after severe intoxication; or are excessive given the amount of cannabis used.

FLASHBACK SYNDROME

Prolonged use of marijuana or hashish can cause flashbacks, which are defined as psychotic experiences from past psychedelic or marijuana experiences (Frances and Franklin, 1994). A flashback is a seemingly realistic recurrence of feelings and perceptions originally experienced under the influence of cannabis (or a psychedelic drug). Most flashbacks are episodes of visual distortion, reexperienced intense emotion, or physical symptoms. Flashbacks generally decrease in number and intensity over time, but in rare cases they become more frequent (Beeder and Millman, 1995).

CHRONIC CANNABIS /AMOTIVATIONAL SYNDROME

An amotivational syndrome has been described in various parts of the world in persons who chronically use high doses of marijuana or hashish. Many of the studies were conducted in Jamaica, India, and Egypt (Frances and Franklin, 1994). Chronic users exhibit apathy, a diminished capacity to carry out long-term plans, an inability to master new problems, and a deterioration of personal hygiene. These users are described as withdrawn, passive, easily distracted, and having poor judgment. Generally, chronic cannabis use leads to impaired memory

Marijuana use may lead to aggressive, violent behavior and conduct disorder. Conduct disorder includes repeated violation of social rules and others' personal rights and can result in delinquency and social problems.

and fatigue, producing a "fog" that lasts several weeks after quitting cannabis use.

Although there is skepticism about the existence of this syndrome, it is clear that heavy cannabis use, by adolescents in particular, tends to stifle ambition and drive and impair school performance. However, some individuals have shown enthusiasm in the pursuit of one particular goal, such as intense involvement with rock or reggae music. In general, chronic heavy cannabis use has been associated with profound changes in perspective, dress, and behavior (Beeder and Millman, 1995).

CANNABIS WITHDRAWAL

Some heavy users of marijuana and hashish who have attempted to quit have experienced irritable or anxious moods accompanied by tremors, marked perspiration, nausea, loss of appetite, and sleep distur-

Heavy penalties for possession of marijuana and other drugs are an attempt to decrease drug use and its associated problems. The Controlled Substance Act of 1970 made possession of marijuana a misdemeanor and the intent to sell or transfer it a felony. In some states, possession of marijuana in small quantities (250 grams or less) can be prosecuted as possession with intent to distribute—a crime that can carry a penalty of up to 10 years in jail.

cent, but they still regard the experiment as a success because use of other drugs has remained at low rates. The rate of cocaine use among Dutch youth, for example, continues to be reported at about 0.3 percent.

CURRENT ISSUES SURROUNDING CANNABIS USE

Recreational use of marijuana and hashish has waxed and waned at different points since the drugs' appearance in the United States more than a century ago, and the 1990s have seen marijuana use rise once again. In fact, drug use overall in the United States has increased dramatically over the past three decades, and the burden on society has been similarly magnified. The medical profession, for example, has seen an increasing number of individuals whose substance abuse either leads to or complicates their reasons for seeking treatment. In addition, there are an inestimable number of other patients whose drug problems may not be identified and thus not be associated with the cause of their visit (Kleber, 1995).

Complicating the problem is cannabis's evolution into a stronger drug that is more easily accessible today. The marijuana available on the streets at the end of the 20th century is more potent, perhaps 10 times as

DRUG DEALING NOT A LUCRATIVE BUSINESS

Television shows and movies often portray drug dealers as rich and powerful, driving luxury automobiles and wearing lots of gold jewelry. But dealing drugs is not an easy way to get rich; in fact, a drug dealer looking for customers outside the local fast-food restaurant may make less than the person flipping burgers inside.

A study by economist Steven Levitt of the University of Chicago and sociologist Sudhir Venkatesh of Harvard University found that the bottom-level dealers make just $3 an hour. The only ones who make money on drugs are the gang leaders, who can make as much as $65 an hour while confining the risks—arrest, murder by a rival gang member—to the low-level pushers. And because of poverty in the inner cities, there are always youths attracted by the glamour of gangs and drugs that are willing to fill these dealer positions.

"There's the mythology that the media has built about the lucrativeness of pushing drugs, but the lessons of introductory economics suggest it can't be true," Levitt told *Forbes* magazine in August 1998. "These are kids with very low skills and there's a reserve army of them waiting to get into the gang. Competition would suggest that the employer [the gang leader] has all the power in this relationship."

Most youths join a gang in hopes of rising to the top of the power structure, and thus achieving the power and money that come with being leader of the gang. However, in the violent world of drug gangs, few ever reach that level. "Right now, the kids are completely getting the calculation wrong about what the likelihood is they're going to rise up in the gang," Venkatesh told *Forbes*. Educating gang members about the drug "business" may lead some of them to take legitimate jobs or inspire them to remain in school and get an education.

Support from family and friends can keep an adolescent who has experimented with drugs off the path to drug dependency or abuse.

strong as it was 20 years earlier. And the combination of a higher rate of usage among teens in the United States and stronger doses of marijuana and hashish adds up to significantly more troublesome effects, in the forms of violence, psychotic behavior, delusions, hallucinations, and other unpredictable, potentially dangerous conduct.

Despite the prevalence of cannabis abuse in our society and the potential dangers it can pose for the user's physical and mental health, many doctors are not adequately trained to treat these problems. Research funds for substance abuse equal about one-tenth of what goes into research on AIDS, cancer, and cardiovascular disease. Although drug abuse may not appear to be as critical a problem as these life-threatening diseases, it nevertheless affects such conditions substantially (Kleber, 1995).

Funding for treatment is also lacking, usually because it is thought that treatment of drug abuse and dependence is ineffective. Research, however, has shown otherwise. In 1994, a study in California found that every dollar put into drug treatment saved the state approximately seven dollars in reduced jail, insurance, hospitalization, and welfare costs. Helping users to overcome their disorder would diminish the harm done to families and society. Preventive measures as well as treatment could thereby greatly reduce the overall burden on society (Kleber and Galanter, 1995).

6

CURRENT TREATMENT OPTIONS

enerally, adolescent use of marijuana and hashish—despite having some adverse effects—does not lead users to seek professional attention. Support, reassurance, and advice from friends or family usually suffice (Frances and Franklin, 1994). Problems resulting from abuse or chronic use of marijuana may require treatment such as the day program attended by Daniel in the following case (more serious cases may need to be admitted to the psychiatric ward of a hospital):

Daniel, a 16-year-old who attended a youth drug-and-alcohol day treatment program, reported having smoked two to three grams of cannabis daily for a year, beginning when he was 14-$^1/_2$ years old. For the six months prior to starting the treatment program, he had increased his daily dose to four to six grams. Daniel had also tried cocaine and LSD but was not a regular user, and he drank about six to eight beers once or twice every two months.

He had tried to stop using cannabis on his own four months prior to his visit. Each time he stopped or reduced his use, within two days he felt ill and often experienced nausea, vomiting, diarrhea, shakiness, agitation, and drug craving. Because of the discomfort, he would start smoking marijuana again to relieve the symptoms. After admission to the chemical dependency day treatment program, Daniel was able to stop his cannabis use.

During the initial 48 hours of being drug free, he again experienced flu-like symptoms, stomach upset, shakiness, and drug craving. Over the next few days he complained of other symptoms, including initial insomnia, headaches, dizziness, irritable moods, and night sweats. The majority of withdrawal symptoms abated within 10 days, with the exception of insomnia and mood irritability. Daniel had several lapses when he again used canabis; however,

Students at a Drug Prevention Fair at a Brooklyn, New York, public school. Programs to discourage drug use before it begins may be an effective way of decreasing drug use among adolescents.

after attending an extended day treatment program, he was eventually able to stop using marijuana altogether (Duffy and Milin, 1996).

EARLY DETECTION

Because of the many ways that excessive marijuana use can disrupt adolescent development, the earlier chronic users are identified, the better. Experimentation with drugs typically starts around 12 or 13 years old, so parents and teachers of middle and junior high school students are usually the adults best able to detect drug use. Involvement, concern, and control by parents have a strong influence on the behavior of very young teenagers. Several years later, parental influence may wane and peer group identification may increase.

The severity of a drug problem—from drug use to dependence to abuse—is often determined by the age of the individual when he or she first starts using drugs. The earlier the onset, the higher the probability that the individual will use drugs frequently or even abuse drugs as an adult. A study called "Monitoring the Future"—an annual survey of about 50,000 students in grades 8, 10, and 12—reveals that adolescents who first used marijuana in the 8th grade exhibit higher use in the 12th grade than those who first used marijuana in the 9th to 12th grades. This study also determined that the importance of peer attitudes varies with respondents' grade at onset of marijuana use. Those who begin using in the eighth grade or before view peer group norms as far more important in their choices than disapproving parental attitudes (Cattarello et al., 1995).

For adolescents who choose to experiment with drugs, intervention by parents, siblings, and friends may be all it takes to stop them from continuing toward abuse or dependence. Once they start abusing drugs, treatment may be required to help them quit.

PHASES OF TREATMENT

Initially, patients tend to deny any health or psychological problems, especially if they have been forced into treatment. Sometimes it is not until they stop using the drug and notice improvement that they admit they have a drug problem. In addition to improving self-awareness, therapy can help adolescent drug users make certain lifestyle changes, such as avoiding those persons, places, and things related to drug use. Those peers with whom the patient associates getting high tend to be too closely—sometimes exclusively—linked to drug use and may have little to offer someone who has stopped using. Effecting such changes in the patient may require attending intervention groups, changing schools, or using a chemical dependency or therapeutic community program (Frances and Franklin, 1994). Several studies suggest that prevention and intervention efforts aimed at the family, the school, and the adolescent's belief system can also prove helpful in reducing the likelihood of associating with delinquent and drug-using peers—which, in turn, should influence actual drug use (Cattarello, 1995).

All phases of treatment have one goal in common for the user: abstinence from drugs. Each person needs to be evaluated to determine which program would be most effective for him or her. Individual therapy may uncover such troublesome issues as poor self-esteem, depression, severe family problems, and psychological disorders. To address these issues, however, family or group therapy may be necessary.

In the "trust fall," an individual falls backwards without putting his arms back or otherwise trying to break his fall, trusting the group to catch him. Learning to trust others is an important component of group therapy.

Parental counseling also may be effective in resolving disturbed family interaction and disciplinary issues (Frances and Franklin, 1994).

CESSATION OF CANNABIS USE

The first step in any treatment program is for the patient to recognize that drug use significantly interferes with his or her life. Patients are encouraged to make a commitment to ceasing drug use. Individuals often show significant denial and sometimes open hostility during this stage, so the therapist's job is to break through the denial and motivate users to change (Beeder and Millman, 1995).

DRUG MONITORING

During the treatment process, periodic screening for marijuana and other drugs is common. Urine tests are generally sufficient to identify the presence of cannabis in the body. Because the by-products remain in bodily fluids for extended periods of time and are excreted slowly, routine urine tests for casual users can be positive for seven to 10 days. Heavy users of cannabis may test positive for two to four weeks. It is important to understand, however, that a positive urine test only shows that cannabis has been used; it does not establish whether the person has a problem with cannabis dependence, abuse, or intoxication. While urine tests can detect the use of cannabis, only blood samples can indicate the level of intoxication (Frances and Franklin, 1994).

OUTPATIENT TREATMENT

Outpatient programs generally provide a range of services from daylong programs to group or individual sessions on a weekly basis. Optimally, during the early phases of treatment, a comprehensive evaluation is made to determine which combination of therapy sessions—including individual therapy, family analysis, group sessions, and educational activities—will most effectively help the patient. Contact with the program initially should be a major focus of the patient's life. As the patient continues to progress, the degree of involvement is reduced and the program becomes more peripheral to his or her daily activities (Beeder and Millman, 1995).

Outpatient treatment is often anchored by a 12 step program similar to that of Alcoholics Anonymous. Group and individual therapy, family therapy, and periodic urine testing (to monitor abstinence from drugs) are the usual supplements to such self-help groups. Adolescent drug programs may concentrate on promoting age-related behavior and increasing communication through various verbal and nonverbal methods. Family therapy helps the patient's parents and siblings to become aware of how they can help (and avoid hindering) the treatment process (Frances and Franklin, 1994).

INDIVIDUAL PSYCHOTHERAPY

Psychiatric therapy may be a crucial treatment option for patients who have cannabis-related problems. Initially, therapists may have difficulty connecting with adolescent patients, as drug-using teens in particular tend to be rebellious and assume an antisocial stance. Once trust is established, however, therapy can move on to address the caus-

Various types of drug treatment programs, such as halfway houses and rehabilitation programs, are available if in-patient treatment is required.

es of the drug abuse.

Although a marijuana-use disorder may bring an adolescent to treatment, marijuana may not be the only drug he or she uses. As marijuana is often used in conjunction with other drugs, therapy can only succeed if the therapist understands whether and to what extent other drugs are involved. For example, a person who abuses cocaine may use marijuana to alleviate some of the anxiety or "wired" feeling caused by the cocaine; marijuana is also used to increase the feelings of intoxication from alcohol (Beeder, 1995).

A patient may also have an accompanying psychological disorder that may have led to or was uncovered by the use of marijuana. Once the person is drug free, individual therapy can help him or her resolve underlying psychological conflicts. Addressing such issues also serves as an effective tool to prevent possible relapse.

FAMILY THERAPY

Adolescents with marijuana problems typically still live with their parents and siblings, and their behavior has a significant impact on family relations. Family therapy may be critical to helping the family learn how to support and encourage the adolescent at home. The family and the therapist attempt to develop a unit that will function as a source of support during the early stages of treatment. These stages often focus on improving communication patterns, altering parental expectations, and addressing parental or sibling drug use. Some therapists encourage family involvement to help eliminate drug-related associations and activities and to develop a productive support network of a carefully selected group of family members and friends.

GROUP THERAPY

Group therapy is the most frequently used treatment for all types of drug abuse, primarily abuse of cannabis. Usually consisting of 10 to 15 adolescents and a counselor, a drug treatment group gives teens the opportunity to deal with their particular issues, aided by group members. Ideally, the group helps teens identify suppressed feelings, see how addiction has hurt themselves and others, and begin to see the need for change. By sharing their feelings and listening to other group members, teens are encouraged to discover who they are. Education on the causes and effects of drug use is often included. Groups are useful for teaching socialization and problem-solving skills and may reduce the sense of isolation that persons who abuse drugs often feel.

TWELVE-STEP PROGRAMS

Treatment procedures modeled after Alcoholics Anonymous's 12-step program have proved useful for many persons who abuse drugs. Members of these groups accept support from a "higher power" in order to kick their addiction and are encouraged to adhere to steps, traditions, and value systems based primarily on sobriety (Beeder and Millman, 1995)

In the past, cannabis-dependent adolescents have not participated extensively in these groups. Recently, however, many meetings of Drugs Anonymous and other self-help groups have become more sensitive to their needs. Whereas 12-step programs encourage adults to continue to think of themselves as recovering addicts, they treat adolescents somewhat differently. After a year or more of abstinence and appropriate social adjustment, young individuals are encouraged to think of themselves as similar to their peers, though with the recognition that they continue to be at increased risk (Beeder and Millman, 1995).

INPATIENT TREATMENT

Dependence on marijuana alone rarely requires a person to be hospitalized or be restricted from access to friends and family. However, inpatient intervention may be necessary in cases involving severe abuse or behavioral problems, especially in teenage populations. Before an individual is admitted to a hospital or clinic, he or she must meet one or more of the following criteria: 1) the inability to cease drug use despite the help of outpatient treatment; 2) the presence of psychological or medical conditions (this is rare) that require close observation and treatment, such as severe depressive symptoms, psychotic states, or extreme debilitation; 3) the absence of adequate psychological and social support groups that might facilitate the cessation of drug use; 4) the necessity to interrupt a living situation that reinforces continued drug taking; or 5) the need to enhance motivation or break through denial.

Once it has been determined that inpatient treatment is necessary, the appropriate program must be chosen to match the needs of the patient. One option, a rehabilitation program, is based on the disease model of chemical dependency. These programs often feature a strong 12-step program component, and groups are usually intensely confrontational. A second, though rarely used, option is the psychiatric hospital, which is reserved for the more severe psychopathological cases. Most cannabis-dependent adolescents would not have symptoms serious enough to be placed in such a setting. For adolescents, the disadvantage of inpatient treatment is that it disrupts their lives and school careers, reinforces their insecurity about their abilities or even their sanity, and often stigmatizes them (Frances and Franklin, 1994).

RESIDENTIAL TREATMENT

Residential treatment is basically a transitional living situation for adolescents who are not yet ready to return home from inpatient treatment. These adolescents may need such a setting either because they didn't make enough progress as an inpatient or because they have an unresolved family issue at home, such as a parent who abuses drugs. Residential treatment is typically referred to as secondary or extended treatment and is set up in two forms: halfway houses and therapeutic communities (Milhorn, 1994).

HALFWAY HOUSES

Halfway houses provide a supportive, drug-free living environment for usually two to six months. The household may have from 10 to 20 adolescents who live together in a supervised setting and share responsibility for maintaining the house. They shop for groceries, cook meals, do housework, and wash their own clothes. Adolescents also attend school during the day and are encouraged to hold a part-time job. Treatment, which is kept at a minimum, typically consists of support group meetings (Milhorn, 1994).

THERAPEUTIC COMMUNITIES

Originally developed to treat heroin addicts, therapeutic communities today focus on multidrug users and adolescents. The communities place an emphasis on patient socialization and offer programs that run from three months to two years. The program comprises a supervised group of adolescents who live in dormitories and learn to work for the betterment of the whole community. They do chores, cook meals, and generally maintain the facility. Some communities require residents to be separated from the outside world; others do not. Varying levels of treatment are found among communities, but group therapy sessions are held and are usually strongly confrontational.

Many therapeutic communities conduct wilderness programs in which adolescents can participate in activities like camping, canoeing, and white-water rafting. In addition to building self-confidence, these experiences demonstrate to adolescents the possibilities of having fun without using drugs (Milhorn, 1994).

■   ■   ■

With the proper treatment, anyone can eliminate marijuana—and the problems it causes—from their life. However, all too often marijuana abuse is not taken as seriously as abuse of other drugs, because its effects are not considered as serious as the effects of illegal substances such as heroin or cocaine. But marijuana is not a harmless drug. As this book illustrates, it can cause many negative effects, including poor performance in school or at work, as well as physical problems such as lung disease or brain damage. From a sociological standpoint, the problem of marijuana abuse, as well as abuse of other drugs, continues to grow.

In addition to treatment, a program of prevention is also needed. This must include education about the danger of drug use. In 1998 the National Office of Drug Control Policy began a new series of television commercials designed to educate children and teens about the effects of drug use. As with the "Just Say No" campaign of the 1980s, it is hoped that this new advertising/education campaign will reduce the rising number of young adults who use illegal substances. Lawmakers, teachers, parents, and counselors must continue to wage the war on drugs.

APPENDIX

FOR MORE INFORMATION

Parents of children and adolescents who have struggled with drug addictions, together with mental health professionals and teachers, have established national organizations that provide education and support for parents, as well as advocacy services and research facilities. Many of these national groups also have local chapters that serve as a powerful adjunct to direct clinical services. The following is a list of organizations and resource centers.

Addiction Research Foundation (ARF)
33 Russell Street
Toronto, Ontario M5S 2S1
Canada

American Counsel for Drug Education
204 Monroe Street
Suite 110
Rockville, MD 20850
(301) 294-0600, (800) 488-DRUG

Center for Substance Abuse Prevention (CSAP)
5600 Fishers Lane
Rockwall II Building
Rockville, MD 20857
(800) 662-HELP

Families in Action, National Drug Abuse Center
3845 North Druid Hills Road
Suite 300
Decatur, GA 30033
(404) 325-5799

Friday Night Live
California Department of Alcohol and Drug Programs
11 Capitol Mall
Room 223
Sacramento, CA 95814
(916) 445-7456

Just Say No Foundation
1777 North California Boulevard.
Room 210
Walnut Creek, CA 94596
(415) 939-6666, (800) 258-2766

National Clearinghouse for Alcohol and Drug Information (NCADI)
P.O. Box 2345
Rockville, MD 20847-2345
(800) 729-6686

National Council on Alcoholism and Drug Dependence (NCADD)
12 West 21st Street
New York, NY 10010
(212) 206-6770

National Families in Action
2296 Henderson Mill Road
Suite 204
Atlanta, GA 30345
(404) 934-6364

National Federation of Parents for Drug-Free Youth
9551 Big Bend
St. Louis, MO 63122
(314) 968-1322

National Institute on Drug Abuse (NIDA)
11400 Rockville Pike
Rockville, MD 20852
(301) 443-1124

National Prevention Network
444 North Capitol Street NW
Suite 642
Washington, DC 20001
(202) 783-6868

Parents Educational Resource Center
1660 South Amphlett Boulevard
Suite 200
San Mateo, CA 94402-2508
(415) 655-2410

Parents Resource Institute for Drug Education, Inc. (PRIDE)
50 Hurt Plaza
Suite 210
Atlanta, GA 30303
(404) 651-2548, (800) 241-7941

STATISTICS

PREVALENCE OF ILLEGAL DRUG USE AMONG 6th-8th, 9th-12th, and 12th GRADE STUDENTS, 1994-95, 1995-96, and 1996-97

Annual Use	1994-95	1995-96	1996-97	Change*	Monthly Use	1994-95	1995-96	1996-97	Change*
Cigarettes					**Cigarettes**				
6th-8th	28.1	31.1	31.8	+0.7 s	6th-8th	15.7	17.2	17.3	+0.1
9th-12th	44.4	48.2	50.2	+2.0 s	9th-12th	31.3	33.4	34.7	+1.3 s
12th	46.8	50.0	52.4	+2.4 s	12th	34.6	36.2	38.3	+2.1 s
Marijuana					**Marijuana**				
6th-8th	9.5	13.6	14.7	+1.1 s	6th-8th	5.7	8.1	8.6	+0.5 s
9th-12th	28.2	34.0	35.8	+1.8 s	9th-12th	18.5	22.3	22.7	+0.4
12th	33.2	37.9	39.4	+1.5 s	12th	20.9	24.3	24.4	+0.1
Cocaine					**Cocaine**				
6th-8th	1.9	2.7	3.0	+0.3 s	6th-8th	1.2	1.5	1.7	+0.2 s
9th-12th	4.5	5.6	5.9	+0.3 s	9th-12th	2.6	2.9	3.0	+0.1
12th	5.3	7.1	7.0	-0.1	12th	2.9	3.6	3.6	+0.0
Uppers					**Uppers**				
6th-8th	3.3	4.6	4.9	+0.3 s	6th-8th	2.0	2.4	2.6	+0.2 s
9th-12th	9.3	10.5	10.3	-0.2	9th-12th	5.1	5.2	5.3	+0.1
12th	10.6	11.6	10.7	-0.9 s	12th	5.6	5.8	5.6	-0.2
Downers					**Downers**				
6th-8th	2.4	3.5	4.0	+0.5 s	6th-8th	1.5	1.9	2.1	+0.2 s
9th-12th	5.5	7.1	7.2	+0.1	9th-12th	3.4	3.8	3.8	+0.0
12th	5.9	7.4	7.4	+0.0	12th	3.6	4.1	3.9	-0.2
Inhalants					**Inhalants**				
6th-8th	6.3	8.5	8.9	+0.4 s	6th-8th	2.9	3.5	3.7	+0.2
9th-12th	7.5	7.6	7.1	-0.5 s	9th-12th	3.5	3.4	3.1	-0.3 s
12th	6.6	6.6	5.8	-0.8 s	12th	3.0	3.1	2.7	-0.4 s
Hallucinogens					**Hallucinogens**				
6th-8th	2.4	3.3	3.6	+0.3 s	6th-8th	1.5	1.8	2.0	+0.2 s
9th-12th	7.7	9.5	9.5	+0.0	9th-12th	4.1	4.5	4.2	-0.3 s
12th	9.7	12.1	11.7	-0.4	12th	4.8	5.1	4.6	-0.5

* Note: Level of significance of difference between the 1995-96 and 1996-97 surveys: s=0.05, using chi-square with variables year and use/no use.

SAMPLE SIZES:	Grade	1994-95	1995-96	1996-97
	6th-8th	92,453	58,596	68,071
	9th-12th	105,788	70,964	73,006
	12th	20,698	14,261	15,532

Source: PRIDE USA Survey 1994–95, 1995–96, and 1996–97.

APPENDIX

SOURCES CITED

Anthony, J. C., A. M. Arria, and E. O. Johnson. "Epidemiological and Public Health Issues for Tobacco, Alcohol, and Other Drugs." *Review of Psychiatry* 14, sec. 1. Washington, D.C.: American Psychiatric Press, 1995.

Beeder, A.B., and R. B. Millman. "Cannabis Abuse and Dependence." *Treatments of Psychiatric Disorders*, 2nd edition. Washington, D.C.: American Psychiatric Press, 1995.

Brook, J. S., M. Whiteman, S. J. Finch, and P. Cohen. "Young Adult Drug Use and Delinquency: Childhood Antecedents and Adolescent Mediators." *Journal of the American Academy of Child and Adolescent Psychiatry* 35, no. 12 (December 1996).

Cattarello, A. M., R. R. Clayton, and C. G. Leukefeld. "Adolescent Alcohol and Drug Abuse," *Review of Psychiatry* 14, sec. 1. Washington, D.C.: American Psychiatric Press, 1995.

Chilcoat, Howard D., and James C. Anthony. "Impact of Parent Monitoring on Initiation of Drug Use through Late Childhood." *Journal of the American Academy of Child and Adolescent Psychiatry* 35, no. 1 (January 1996).

Clark, Robert R. "Marijuana Use Associated with First Episode of Psychiatric Illness in an Adolescent Population." *American Journal on Addictions* 3, no. 1 (Winter 1994).

Duffy, Anne, and Robert Milin. "Case Study: Withdrawal Syndrome in Adolescent Chronic Cannabis Users." *Journal of the American Academy of Child and Adolescent Psychiatry* 35, no. 12 (December 1996).

Dupre, Deirdre, Norman Miller, Mark Gold, and Kathy Rospenda. "Initiation and Progression of Alcohol, Marijuana, and Cocaine Use Among Adolescent Abusers." *American Journal on Addictions* 4, no. 1 (Winter 1995).

Frances, R. J., and J. E. Franklin, Jr. "Alcohol and Other Psychoactive Substance Use Disorders." *APP Textbook of Psychiatry*, 2nd edition.

Sources Cited

Washington, D.C.: American Psychiatric Press, 1994.

Kandel, Denise, and Mark Davies. "High School Students Who Use Crack and Other Drugs." *Archives of General Psychiatry* 53, no. 1 (January 1996).

Kay, Paul. Letter to the Editor: "Experience with Risk-Taking Adolescents." *Journal of the American Academy of Child and Adolescent Psychiatry* 35, no. 11 (November 1996).

Kleber, H. "Substance Abuse." *Review of Psychiatry* 14. Washington, D.C.: American Psychiatric Press, 1995.

Kleber, H., and M. Galanter. "Substance-related Disorders." *Treatments of Psychiatric Disorders*, 2nd ed. Washington, D.C.: American Psychiatric Press, 1995.

Mezzich, Ada Castillo, et al. "Gender Differences in the Pattern and Progression of Substance Use in Conduct-Disordered Adolescents." *American Journal on Addictions* 3, no. 4 (Fall 1994).

McGlashan, T. H., and Krystal, J. H. "Schizophrenia-related Disorders and Dual Diagnosis." *Treatments of Psychiatric Disorders*, 2nd edition. Washington, D.C.: American Psychiatric Press, 1995.

Milhorn, Harold T., Jr. Drug and Alcohol Abuse: *The Authoritative Guide for Parents, Teachers, and Counselors*. New York: Plenum Press, 1994.

Moss, Howard, and Ralph Tarter. "Substance Abuse, Aggression, and Violence." *American Journal on Addictions* 2, no. 2 (Spring 1993).

National Institute on Drug Abuse. "Director's Report to the National Advisory Council on Drug Abuse," 1996. [On-line] Available: www.nida.nih.gov.

Royce, J. E., and D. Scratchley. *Alcoholism and Other Drug Problems*. New York: The Free Press, 1996.

Walter, H. J., "Substance Abuse and Substance Use Disorders." *Treatments of Psychiatric Disorders*, 2nd edition. Washington, D.C.: American Psychiatric Press, 1995.

Westermeyer, Joseph. Letter to the Editor. *American Journal of Psychiatry* 149, no. 12 (December 1992).

Anorexia: an eating disorder characterized by refusal to eat enough to maintain a healthy weight, extreme weight loss, and loss of menstruation in females.

Anxiety disorder: any of a group of psychological disorders characterized by extreme stress, nervousness, or anxiety in situations that should not cause such severe reactions. Anxiety disorders can be triggered or worsened by use of marijuana.

Bulimia: an eating disorder characterized by repeated episodes of binging, or drastic overeating, and purging by forced vomiting or laxative abuse.

Cannabis: the plant from which marijuana and hashish are made, originally native to India.

Flashbacks: a symptom of chronic drug use in which a user who is not intoxicated experiences effects of intoxication for a brief period. Flashbacks are most common with hallucinogens such as LSD but have been known to occur in marijuana users as well.

Gateway effect: a contested theory which states that users of marijuana are more likely than non-users to go on to try other illegal drugs.

Hashish: concentrated resin made from the flowering tops of the female hemp plant; a more potent drug from the same source as marijuana.

Hemp: the plant *Cannabis sativa,* from which marijuana and hashish are made. Hemp can also be used for other purposes, such as cloth fibers, paper-making, fuel, and food.

Joint: one of the most common street names for a marijuana cigarette. Other names for the drug include "weed," "pot," "reefer," "grass," and "mary-jane."

Marijuana: a drug derived primarily from the leaves and flowering tops of the female hemp plant, which are dried and smoked.

Mood disorders: a group of psychological disorders, including depression and manic depression, characterized by extreme mood swings that impair a person's ability to function normally in society and which can, in severe cases, drive someone to attempt suicide. Marijuana use may exacerbate previously unnoticed mood disorder symptoms.

PCP: phencyclidine, or "angel dust," a large-animal tranquilizer sometimes used to lace marijuana. PCP has hallucinogenic effects on humans and can cause users to have sudden violent or self-destructive episodes.

THC: delta-9-tetrahydrocannabinol, the chemical in the cannabis plant that is largely responsible for the psychoactive effects of marijuana and hashish. The THC content in marijuana averages around 5 percent, while in hashish it can range up to almost 15 percent.

Therapeutic community: a treatment option originally developed for heroin users but now common to multidrug and adolescent drug addicts, in which patients live in a structured, drug-free environment where they receive therapy and learn how to socialize and have productive lives without using drugs.

APPENDIX

FURTHER READING

American Psychiatric Association. *The Diagnostic and Statistical Manual of Mental Disorders*, 4th edition. Washington, D.C.: The American Psychiatric Press, 1994.

———. *DSM-IV Sourcebook*, 3 vols. Washington, D.C.: The American Psychiatric Press, 1996.

———. *Textbook of Psychiatry*, 2nd edition. Washington, D.C.: The American Psychiatric Press, 1995.

———. *Treatment of Psychological Disorders*, 2nd edition, 2 vols. Washington, D.C.: The American Psychiatric Press, 1995.

Galperin, Anne. *Marijuana: Its Effects on Mind and Body*. New York: Chelsea House Publishers, 1992.

Grinspoon, Lester, and James B. Bakalar. *Marihuana, the Forbidden Medicine*. New Haven: Yale University Press, 1997.

Mathre, Mary Lynn, ed. *Cannabis in Medical Practice: A Legal, Historical, and Pharmacological Overview of the Therapeutic Use of Marijuana*. New York: McFarland & Co., 1997.

Savage, J. C. *Cash Crop: A Closer Look Inside the Outdoor Marijuana Growing Business*. Superior, Wis.: Savage Press, 1991.

Schleichert, Elizabeth. *Marijuana*. Springfield, N.J.: Enslow Publishers, 1996.

Zimmer, Lynn, and John P. Morgan. *Marijuana Myths, Marijuana Facts: A Review of the Scientific Evidence*. New York: Lindesmith Center, 1997.

APPENDIX

INDEX

Index

APPENDIX

PICTURE CREDITS

page

8: Kathy Sloane/Photo Researchers, Inc.
12: UPI/Corbis-Bettmann
14: Courtesy Drug Enforcement Agency
16: Michael Austin/Photo Researchers, Inc.
19: UPI/Corbis-Bettmann
22: George Turner/Photo Researchers, Inc.
24: UPI/Corbis-Bettmann
27: AP/Wide World Photos
30: Spencer Grant/Photo Researchers, Inc.
32: Bill Bachman/Photo Researchers, Inc.
34: Bonnie Freer/Photo Researchers, Inc.
36: Cynthia Dopkin/Photo Researchers, Inc. (top); Barbara Rios/Photo Researchers, Inc. (bottom)
40: Photo Researchers, Inc.

43: Shirley Zeiberg Photography
45: Shirley Zeiberg Photography
46: Jan Halaska/Photo Researchers, Inc.
49: Laimute Druskis/Photo Researchers, Inc.
50: Shirley Zeiberg Photography
52: Barbara Rios/Photo Researchers, Inc.
54: James Stevenson/Photo Researchers, Inc.
58: Van Bucher/Photo Researchers, Inc.
60: © 1995 Terry Wild Studio
63: © 1994 Terry Wild Studio
66: Shirley Zeiberg Photography
68: David M. Grossman/Photo Researchers, Inc.
70: Bill Bachman/Photo Researchers, Inc.
72: Hubertus Kanus/Photo Researchers, Inc.

Senior Consulting Editor Carol C. Nadelson, M.D., is president and chief executive officer of the American Psychiatric Press, Inc., staff physician at Cambridge Hospital, and Clinical Professor of Psychiatry at Harvard Medical School. In addition to her work with the American Psychiatric Association, which she served as vice president in 1981-83 and president in 1985-86, Dr. Nadelson has been actively involved in other major psychiatric organizations, including the Group for the Advancement of Psychiatry, the American College of Psychiatrists, the Association for Academic Psychiatry, the American Association of Directors of Psychiatric Residency Training Programs, the American Psychosomatic Society, and the American College of Mental Health Administrators. In addition, she has been a consultant to the Psychiatric Education Branch of the National Institute of Mental Health and has served on the editorial boards of several journals. Doctor Nadelson has received many awards, including the Gold Medal Award for significant and ongoing contributions in the field of psychiatry, the Elizabeth Blackwell Award for contributions to the causes of women in medicine, and the Distinguished Service Award from the American College of Psychiatrists for outstanding achievements and leadership in the field of psychiatry.

Consulting Editor Claire E. Reinburg, M.A., is editorial director of the American Psychiatric Press, Inc., which publishes about 60 new books and six journals a year. She is a graduate of Georgetown University in Washington, D.C., where she earned bachelor of arts and master of arts degrees in English. She is a member of the Council of Biology Editors, the Women's National Book Association, the Society for Scholarly Publishing, and Washington Book Publishers.

As director of Write Stuff Editorial Service in New York City, **Elizabeth Russell Connelly** has written and edited for medical and business journals, trade magazines, high-tech firms, and various book publishers. She earned an MBA from New York University's Stern School in 1993 and a certificate in language studies from Freiburg Universitaet (Switzerland) in 1985. Her published work includes a global studies book for young adults; more than 14 Access travel guides covering North America, the Caribbean, and Europe; and several volumes in Chelsea House Publishers' Encyclopedia of Psychological Disorders.